"The TM technique has helped our career and our personal life more than anything else. Our creativity has blossomed, sickness has virtually disappeared and we have more energy than we ever dreamed of. But most importantly, with the removal of the stress from our nervous systems, our eyes have opened to the beautiful wonders of creation, and we enjoy each day as if it were real magic."

Debbie and Doug Henning
World Famous Magicians

"Leaders in all walks of life know that intangibles such as intuition, courage, a sense of justice, imagination, clarity of thought, and good fortune are essential to success. It is precisely these intangibles which we who practice the Transcendental Meditation program enjoy in our lives in growing abundance."

Susan Gore
Director, W.L. Gore & Associates
Multi-national high technology
manufacturing enterprise

"In 1982 I was looking to revitalize my company, and I decided to implement the Transcendental Meditation program. Within a year 73% of our employees learned the TM technique through our company sponsored program. Absenteeism is now down 89% . Productivity has increased 52%. Sales are up 120%. And profits are up 520% from 1982 — an all-time high. If another CEO asks me how we did it, I tell him, 'TM — my best business decision.' "

Raoul W. Montgomery, Jr.
President, H.A. Montgomery Co.
Chemical manufacturing company
and supplier to the automotive
industry for 60 years

Will this book teach me how to do TM?

This book will tell you what the Transcendental Meditation program is, and why you might like to enjoy the TM technique. But you must learn the TM technique personally from a trained teacher, who will guide you on the basis of your own experience as you learn the technique.

There are over 10,000 teachers of the Transcendental Meditation program in the U.S. alone,with TM centers called Capitals of the Age of Enlightenment in nearly every city.

Why do you keep referring to the TM technique and the TM program? I thought it was all just TM.

The TM *technique* is a specific, scientific practice. The TM *program* includes twice-daily practice of the TM technique and other educational services, which we will talk about later (chapter 4). "Transcendental Meditation" and "TM" identify the specific educational programs offered only by the various nonprofit organizations authorized by Maharishi.

Therefore, participating in programs identified by these terms assures you of receiving the techniques, programs and benefits that are described in this book and verified by scientific research conducted around the world.

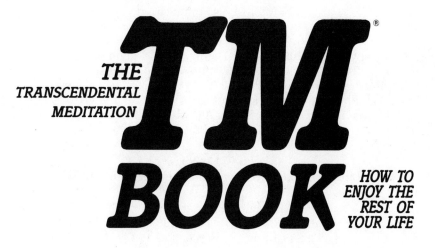

THE TRANSCENDENTAL MEDITATION TM® BOOK
HOW TO ENJOY THE REST OF YOUR LIFE

New Edition

Denise Denniston
Illustrated by Barry Geller

The TM Book: How to Enjoy the Rest of Your Life

New Edition

A Fairfield Press Publication

Text Copyright © 1975 Denise Denniston and Peter McWilliams
Text Copyright © 1986, 1987 Denise Denniston
Illustrations Copyright © 1975, 1986, 1987 Barry Geller
Photograph on page 9 © 1975 Victor Raymond
Charts used by permission of Age of Enlightenment Press
and MIU Press

ISBN 0-931783-02-X
Library of Congress catalogue number 85-62810

1st printing	January 1986
2nd printing	March 1987
3rd printing	September 1987

Published by Fairfield Press Inc.
P.O. Box 773, Fairfield, Iowa 52556

Product Development by Cobb/Dunlop Publisher Services, Inc.

Distributed by Publishers Group West
5855 Beaudry St., Emeryville, CA 94608
800-982-8319

and by

Age of Enlightenment Press
5000 14th Street, NW, Washington, DC 20011

For individual copies and international inquiries,
please write to Fairfield Press

World Plan, Science of Creative Intelligence, SCI, Transcendental Meditation, TM, TM-Sidhi,
Vedic Science, Maharishi Technology of the Unified Field, are the service marks of WPEC-U.S.
MIU and Maharishi are the service marks of Maharishi International University
Maharishi Ayurveda Medical Center is the service mark of
Maharishi Ayurvedic Corporation of America

TABLE OF CONTENTS

We are delighted to thank all those who helped in the preparation of this book, particularly: Allen Cobb, Bob Cobb, David Dunlop, Stan Crowe, Myron Feld, Nan Geller, Mary Jo Kaiser, Peter Muldavin and Mike Smith.

And for the new edition: Robert Roth, Dell Abrams, Vaughn and Lyn Abrams, Mike Davis, Nat and Marilyn Goldhaber, David and Connie Huebner, Shepley Hansen, Meredith Jacobsen, Barry and Jaine Pitt, Dean Ragland, Jenni Roney, Susan Roth, Thomas Selleck, Michael Sternfeld and Gerald Swanson.

Our own Transcendental Meditation teachers: Terry Gustafson and Bob Markowitz.

and Jerry Jarvis, for all his help, and especially for coming up with eight-elevenths of the title.

About the authors:

Denise Denniston became a teacher of the TM program in 1971. Since then she has taught TM in Omaha, Nebraska, Los Angeles, California and New York City. She has worked at the United States National Center and at the International Capital of the Age of Enlightenment in Europe. She is a Ph.D. Candidate in Philosophy of Education at the University of California at Berkeley, and an adjunct faculty member of Maharishi International University.

Barry Geller, who illustrated this book, was head of the design department of Maharishi International University Press, the international production facility for the TM movement in Europe. He now operates his own freelance advertising, illustration and design business.

This book is dedicated
with profound love
and deepest gratitude to
MAHARISHI MAHESH YOGI
Founder of the
Science of Creative Intelligence
and chief proponent of its practical aspect,
the Transcendental Meditation program

I keep hearing about the Transcendental Meditation program. Why is it becoming so popular?

The Transcendental Meditation (or TM) technique was introduced to the United States by Maharishi Mahesh Yogi in 1959. People started the TM technique, liked it, and told their friends, who started and in turn told their friends, who then also started. Students especially appreciated the value of Maharishi's message: "Man is born to enjoy, to create, and to radiate happiness." By the end of the 1960's, hundreds of thousands of people were practicing the TM technique. The reason most of these people began is because their friends had recommended it.

Then, in 1970, Dr. Robert Keith Wallace of the U.S. began scientific research into the effects of the Transcendental Meditation technique on the mind and body. In his first set of experiments he discovered that during the TM technique, the metabolic rate is reduced by 16% in a matter of minutes. During sleep the metabolic rate is usually reduced by only 12% over a period of many hours. This means that the TM technique quickly provides a state of rest that is much deeper than sleep. These findings were made even more remarkable by the fact that the mind remains alert and awake during this rest—that there is no loss of consciousness as there is during sleep. Dr. Wallace called this unique state of mind and body functioning "restful alertness."

Scientists the world over began studying the effects of the TM technique. The results of these studies, printed in dozens of scientific journals and reported in hundreds of newspapers and magazines, have been responsible for the increasing interest in the TM program over the past few years. These scientific studies offer a vision of man with greater clarity of mind, improved health, and freedom from tension, anxiety, stress. The Transcendental Meditation program changes the quality of life from poverty, emptiness, and suffering to abundance, fulfillment, and happiness.

Excuse my skepticism, but that sounds hopelessly idealistic.

Only a few years ago diseases such as polio and smallpox (not to mention cholera, diphtheria, typhus, typhoid, and whooping cough) were accepted as part of the human condition. Those who thought otherwise were considered hopelessly idealistic. Then came the discovery of vaccines. Today, wherever the vaccines are used, these diseases are no longer found.

The TM technique is practical. Science has proven that it provides deep rest, removes tension and fatigue, and increases mental clarity and intelligence. (More of the scientific results later.) The TM technique is a great scientific discovery. It makes suffering in life a thing of the past. By the end of the book we hope you'll agree that it's not that idealistic after all.

I've heard how difficult meditation is, with concentration and exercises, and I know I could never make my mind a blank.

Neither could we. There are many misconceptions about the words "transcendental" and "meditation." People have the idea that "transcendental" has something to do with Thoreau and Emerson and Walden Pond, and most people are sure that "meditation" involves severe concentration, brown rice diets, pretzel postures—and wasn't there that swami on "You Asked For It!" who sat on nails and ate glass? It would help our understanding to discuss the many things that the TM program is *not*.

Alright. What is not the Transcendental Meditation program?

Excellent question!

Chapter 1

What the TM Program Is Not

TM IS NOT...

RUNNING · JOGGING · RACE WALKING
EVENING STROLL · ISOMETRICS
AEROBICS · FISHING · SITTING UNDER
A TREE · LISTENING TO MUSIC ·
VITAMINS · KNITTING A SWEATER
CATNAPPING · EATING CHOCOLATES
FASTING · READING A BOOK · WATCHING
THE NEWS · BAKING BREAD · WATERING
THE GARDEN · PAINTING A PICTURE
THINKING PLEASANT THOUGHTS
ETC., ETC., ETC.

Is the TM technique the same as jogging?

No. It's not the same as running, jogging, racewalking, an evening stroll, isometrics, aerobics, fishing, sitting under a tree, listening to music, taking vitamins, knitting a sweater, catnapping, eating chocolates, fasting, reading a book, watching the 6:00 news, baking bread, watering the garden, painting a picture, tinkering in the garage, practicing piano, closing your eyes for 10 minutes before work or during a meeting or at the end of the day, organizing your thoughts, thinking pleasant thoughts, or clearing your mind of thoughts. It's none of the above.

Each of these activities may develop some particular facet of our life: jogging provides exercise; knitting produces an afgan. The TM technique is holistic. It is a simple, effortless, natural mental process for unfolding the full potential of the mind, body and emotions. It opens the mind to the field of pure creative intelligence and provides the body with the deepest, most profound rest possible. On the basis of this 20 minute experience twice a day, jogging, aerobics, knitting a sweater, organizing your thoughts — everything becomes far more enjoyable and far more worthwhile.

The TM program is preparation for activity. The nice thing is, after TM we don't need to do things to get rid of stress; we do things because we really enjoy them. Actually, we don't have to do anything to get rid of stress. We do whatever we do because we choose to, because we enjoy it, and because it's beneficial to our life. That's freedom in life. That's true happiness.

natural, no belief needed

GRAVITY GROWTH

ELECTRICITY CALORIES

Do I have to believe in TM for it to work?

No, not at all.

Will it work any better if I do?

No.

Why?

Because the TM process is completely natural.

What do you mean by natural?

That means that it makes use of the natural tendency of the mind to move toward a field of greater charm, and the natural mechanisms of the body to neutralize stress and restore balance in its functioning. It is like gravity. Let's say I don't understand Newton's law of gravity, or that I don't believe in it. Nevertheless, I'm still found sitting in this chair, subject to the law of gravity. If I throw a tennis ball in the air it will fall subject to the law of gravity. And if you do happen to believe in gravity, your tennis ball would not fall any faster than mine.

Natural processes and our intellectual understanding about them are two entirely different matters. Gravity doesn't care whether we believe in it or not. It still works!

In the same way, the TM technique works automatically, spontaneously and effortlessly, according to the laws of nature. Whether or not we believe or understand the intellectual principles behind the technique, it's natural and works the same for everybody.

the **TM** program
does NOT
involve
religious
beliefs

The TM program is not a religion? I've heard it was just some Westernized form of Hinduism.

No, no—it's absurd to assume that just because the TM technique comes from India it must be some Hindu practice. Italy is considered a Catholic country. Galileo, an Italian, discovered that the earth is round. The fact that the earth is round is no more connected with the Catholic Church than the TM technique is connected with the Hindu religion. The TM technique is a scientific discovery which happens to come from India. As with all scientific discoveries, it works everywhere because it involves the basic laws of nature. The TM program does not involve any religious belief or practice — Hindu or otherwise. Just like bathing always works to get you clean, the TM program is a universally applicable practice for getting the most out of life.

Isn't Maharishi a monk?

Yes, he is. Many great scientists and thinkers are men of profound religious convictions. Gregor Mendel, who discovered the laws of genetics, was himself a Jesuit priest. Einstein often spoke of his "cosmic religious sense." A scientist's personal religious beliefs have no bearing on the validity of his contributions to science.

Does TM conflict with any form of religion?

No. People of any religion practice the TM technique. In fact, they find the increased clarity of mind brought about through the TM program greatly broadens the comprehension and enhances the appreciation of their individual religious practices. Priests practice it, rabbis practice it, ministers practice it, and they recommend the TM program to their congregations.

Rabbi Raphael Levine
Rabbi Emeritus of Temple De Hirsh Sinai
Seattle, Washington

"The TM program is not a religion. It has nothing to do with religion except as the easiest technique I have yet discovered for making religion become more alive, more meaningful, by helping people to live the way their religion teaches them to live — on the level of love and self-giving.

"What impresses me about the TM technique is its simplicity. Instead of concentration, contemplation or strenuous self-disciplining exercises to subdue the self-centeredness which we have always believed is our human nature, the TM technique is effortless and enjoyable, practiced twenty minutes twice a day, achieving this miracle for us not by the disciplines of self-denial, but by the joy and happiness of self-enlargement, the enlargement of our state of consciousness; and the miracle is that it works!"

Rev. Kevin P. Joyce
Faculty, St. Joseph College Seminary
Mountain View, California

"Throughout my entire life, I have sought to grow in my commitment as a Christian. About fifteen years ago, I learned the TM technique and have found it to be of enormous value in my Christian life. Even though it is a purely mechanical mental technique which may be practiced by anyone, regardless of religion, I and many thousands of other Christians report that our love for God and neighbor and our devotion to Christ has expanded through the TM practice.

"There are some Christians who wonder how the TM program relates with Christianity. For me personally, all the questions regarding TM and Christianity are answered simply and directly by Jesus himself. He warned that false prophets would appear, usually from within the ranks of Christians themselves (cf. Matthew 7: 21-22). He gave clear criteria by which to judge a person or teaching: 'You will know them by their deeds. Do you ever pick grapes from thornbushes, or figs from prickly plants? Never! Any sound tree bears good fruit, while a decayed tree bears bad fruit...You can tell a tree by its fruit' (Matthew 7: 15-20). And what is the fruit of the Holy Spirit? 'Love, joy, peace, patience, kindness, goodness, faithfulness, gentleness, self-control' (Galatians 5: 22).

"Maharishi's and the TM program's sole desire is to relieve human suffering and to help people to develop their full God-given potential. Just as Christians may and should take advantage of educational and medical resources, so too may they enjoy the TM and TM-Sidhi programs with full assurance that the Lord wants us to do everything possible to care for the temple of his Spirit which we are (1 Corinthians 6: 19). All one need do is glance through the hundreds of scientific studies conducted on TM at leading medical schools and research institutions to see that the technique is 100% beneficial for mind, body, spirit, and environment. 'You can tell a tree by its fruits.' "

21

The Rev. Dr. John Reigstad
Lutheran Clergyman
St. Paul's Lutheran Church, Meriden, Minnesota

"As a Lutheran clergyman, I feel a deep concern for the spiritual development of people around the world. In expressing my concern, I have carefully studied the TM technique, and if it could be used beneficially by Christians. My article, *On the Theological Permissibility of the Psychotherapeutic Use of Transcendental Meditation in a Christian Context'*, carefully documents several important facts: 1) TM can provide significant health benefits for many people, including normalization of body weight and decreased dependency upon tobacco and alcohol; 2) The TM technique is taught as a scientific procedure, and its practice has no necessary religious implications; and 3) Christians need feel no conflict between the practice of the TM technique and the Christian life.

"I have studied scores of meditation strategies, and I have no doubt that TM is the most well-researched technique available. I am especially impressed by the precise teaching procedures which insure that one receives the benefits of the practice.

"I appreciate the concerns of Christians in these matters, and I welcome questions about TM and its role in a Christian context."

What about atheists?

Atheists enjoy the Transcendental Meditation program for the same reason the devoutly religious enjoy it—it involves no dogma, belief, or philosophy. The technique is purely scientific and produces scientifically verifiable results.

But doesn't meditation have something to do with knowing God? Doesn't that make the TM program essentially a religious practice?

The TM program has something to do with knowing *anything*. It makes the mind more orderly, gives the body deep rest, and improves the coordination between the two. This means that with clear awareness we can focus sharply and succeed in activity — whatever our activity may be.

Aren't most who practice the TM program vegetarians?

Some are. Many aren't. But then, a lot of nonTMer's are vegetarians, too. The point is, there are no dietary restrictions involved with the TM program.

No daily ration of brown rice?

Nope.

I can still eat Big Macs?

You can eat anything you want.

This is sounding better and better.

no special clothing

No funny clothes?

No.

How about sandals? Some TM people wear sandals.

And some wear sneakers, or Hush Puppies, or Guccis. We get all kinds. People who enjoy the TM program grow to express their own unique individuality, and this is reflected in their life style, self-expression, and, of course, their clothing.

Oh yes! These are yoga postures, aren't they? What do they have to do with the TM technique?

Nothing. These are hatha yoga postures. The word "hatha" means "force"; "yoga" means "union." Postures are physical and require effort. Hatha yoga can be enjoyable, but deep rest and normalizing of the whole nervous system come most quickly and easily through the Transcendental Meditation technique. The technique is an effortless, natural, mental practice that accomplishes the goal of "yoga" (complete integration of the mind, body, and activity) in the most comfortable, effortless way.

Don't the postures accomplish integration?

Exercises certainly can help improve one's health. But since every aspect of physical health depends on the mind and the nervous system, for complete and natural integration of life we need the TM technique. The key factor recommending the TM program is that it gets to the basis of all our mental and physical functioning. There are many ways of traveling from New York to Los Angeles: walking, bicycling, driving—the TM program is like taking a jet, first class: it's the fastest and most comfortable.

the **TM** technique
is not
contemplation

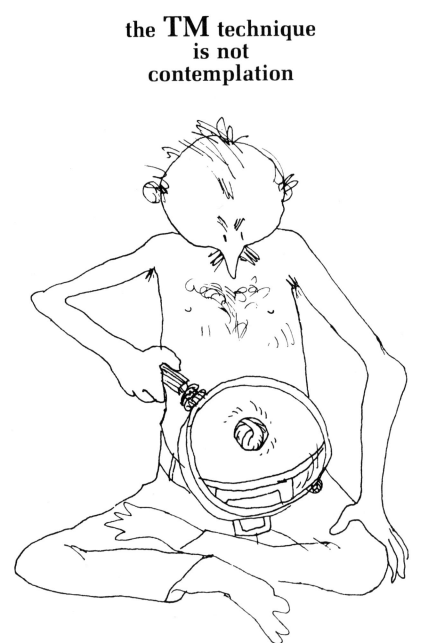

What is contemplation?

Contemplation is thinking *about* something (a problem, a philosophical idea) or just letting the mind wander from one idea to the next with no particular direction.

Isn't that what people mean by "meditation"?

Many do, yes. They say "I am meditating" on this or that thought. Some call quiet reflection "meditation," while others glorify their day-dreams with the title "meditation."

The Transcendental Meditation technique is a very specific practice, very different from any of these sorts of "meditation."

no concentration

How is concentration different from contemplation?

Concentration is the rigid fixing of the mind on one particular point, and holding the attention on this point for as long as possible.

My friend had me stare into a candle for the better part of an hour one night.

Yes, a candle is a common concentration point.

It gave me a headache.

Yes, that is a common result.

And the TM technique involves no concentration?

Absolutely *not!*

In the TM technique, isn't one asked to focus on a mantra?

No. A mantra is given during personal instruction (more of this on pages 185 and 190) but one is not asked to *focus* upon it. To control the use of the mantra in any way is a form of concentration, and concentration is *not* part of the TM technique.

the **TM** technique
is not
bio-feedback
or
alpha-wave
control

Is the TM technique the same as bio-feedback?

No. Bio-feedback is a process whereby a person learns to control some aspect of the body's functioning which is usually not under conscious control — for example, the heart rate, circulation, or brain activity. This is done by connecting some light or sound with what is being controlled so that the subject can see or hear what his body is doing. and learn to change the light or tone by changing the physiology.

There are two major differences between the TM technique and bio-feedback. First, the TM technique is completely effortless. Everything that happens, happens spontaneously, unlike bio-feedback, which requires conscious control and effort to produce some specific change. The changes in the body and mind during the TM technique come without our willing them or learning to do them.

Second, and even more important, the TM technique produces far more than one specific change such as more alpha waves. It produces a spontaneous state of deep rest and alertness for the body and the mind. This shows up as an integrated physiological response that includes a whole *pattern* of brainwave activity. The brain waves found during the TM technique (including alpha) reflect the unique restful alertness that improves the functioning of every aspect of the mind, the body, and the emotions. It produces these changes simultaneously, in a completely balanced way.

Alpha waves?

Alpha waves are a specific frequency of brain waves, or the electrical activity of the brain, measured on the electroencephalograph (EEG) machine. Since some research several years ago connected alpha waves with meditation, tranquility and subjective good feelings, bio-feedback has been used to train people to produce more alpha activity. Although restfulness does produce alpha, alpha doesn't necessarily produce much restfulness. It doesn't work both ways.

no change of life style

No change of life style?

There is no need to change in any way to start the TM program. You simply take the technique home with you, practice it twice a day, and enjoy.

So my life would go on without change.

Without *forcing* change. Life is always changing. The TM program produces remarkably rapid growth. Your life will continue to change naturally, in the direction of more strength, more effectiveness, and more enjoyment. But remember, your own growth is your responsibility every step of the way.

There is no need to change anything to start the TM program?

Right.

chapter 2

What the TM Technique Is

Now that I know what the TM program is not, tell me what the TM technique is.

Let's give you a complete definition first; then we can analyze it point by point.

The Transcendental Meditation technique is a simple, natural, effortless process that allows the mind to experience subtler and subtler levels of the thinking process until thinking is transcended and the mind comes into direct contact with the source of thought.

But please remember that the TM technique produces an experience, and like any experience it is hard to describe or define. No matter how clearly or cleverly we might describe a strawberry, for instance, you would still have only an abstract idea of the strawberry. But when you see a strawberry, feel a strawberry, and taste a strawberry, then the experience becomes very real.

The source of thought. What's that?

Have you ever had the feeling that thoughts don't just spring to the mind fully formed?

I've never thought about it.

Consider it for a moment. Do thoughts simply pop into the mind, fully formed, or do they seem to come from somewhere deep within the mind, existing at some abstract, more subtle level before they become totally clear?

Well, they're not just there. I guess they do seem to come from someplace.

They seem to come from somewhere within us.

All these thoughts come from one source: a field of pure energy deep within the mind.

You're getting a bit abstract, aren't you?

Let us be abstract just a minute longer, because what we want to find out is what the source of thought is really like.

Every thought has some meaning, some direction. Even a nonsensical thought or a thought in a dream makes some kind of sense to us—we recognize it as a picture, as words, as an emotion, or as an idea. This means that every thought has some kind of intelligent purpose or direction. We don't think at random because thoughts themselves contain intelligence.

So now we know one thing about the source of thought—it has to be creative, a reservoir of intelligence. Every bit of intelligence that we display in our daily lives reflects the intelligence contained in our thoughts.

Also, we experience thousands of thoughts every day—they just keep coming and coming. So they must be coming from a virtually unlimited source of energy.

The source of thought, then, is the source of millions of individual bundles of creativity, intelligence, and energy.

42

Some people don't seem to display as much intelligence as they might.

Right. We all display different degrees of intelligence in different kinds of activity. That's why we're talking about the TM program—all of us want to display *maximum* intelligence in *everything* we do. Thinking is the basis of action, action is the basis of achievement, and achievement makes us feel fulfilled.

This still seems abstract . . .

Consider it from the scientific point of view. According to physics, everything that exists is built up of layers of energy, one inside another. Einstein demonstrated that matter is just another form of energy with his equation "$E = mc^2$." Also, we notice that in all creation, from the growth of the plants to the movement of the planets, there is great order, or intelligence. Since thoughts also exist, they must be made of the most basic form of energy as well. And they have their source, or basis, in the same field of creative intelligence and energy that underlies all creation.

What does this have to do with the TM technique?

The regular practice of the Transcendental Meditation technique taps this field of energy within ourselves, bringing it out to fully enhance our lives. We tap the source of intelligence, and daily we are more intelligent. We tap the source of energy, and daily we are more energetic. We tap the source of creativity, and daily we are more creative. So the TM technique is a process by which one contacts this source of pure creativity and intelligence at the basis of the thinking process, allowing this creative intelligence to be expressed in greater clarity of mind, greater efficiency of action, and increasingly fulfilling achievements in daily life.

the TM program
is natural

It sounds very complicated.

It *sounds* complicated, but *doing* it isn't. That's because it's perfectly natural. The mind finds contact with this field of pure creative intelligence highly enjoyable. We are naturally drawn toward that which makes us happiest. Friends, loved ones, music—the mind automatically chooses that which gives the most pleasure. To be drawn toward what we enjoy is very natural.

If it's so natural, why do I have to learn it?

Speaking is natural, yet we had to learn how to speak. There is a certain technique to speaking, but once we learn the technique it all seems quite natural. And it *is* quite natural.

To directly contact the source of our own creativity and intelligence is the most natural thing we can do. All we need is the technique.

the TM technique is easy

the TM technique is effortless

"Easy" and "effortless"?

Anything that is natural *must* be easy and effortless. It is easy to talk, to eat, to sleep, to enjoy our friends—and because it is so easy it's also effortless. The same is true of the TM technique. Once the technique is learned, the process flows—easily and effortlessly.

Ah! There's the catch! "Once the technique is learned." Just how many years does it take to learn this technique?

Years? Days. Hours, actually. Four two-hour sessions with a qualified teacher of the TM program, and that's it.

And then I do the TM technique whenever I want?

No. The TM technique is practiced twice a day, morning and evening, for 15–20 minutes each time. It's preparation for activity. We sit comfortably anywhere we happen to be: propped up in bed, on a train, in the office, in your living room, anywhere.

This twice—daily practice of the TM technique forms the basis of the TM program.

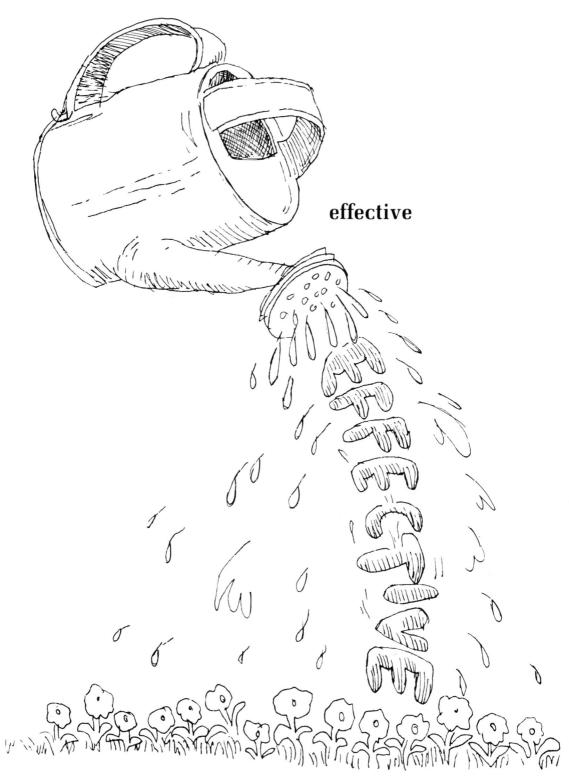

effective

The TM program?

The Transcendental Meditation program fits into your life something like this:

You wake in the morning wishing that sleep had worked a little better. You begin your morning session of the TM technique and contact the source of creative intelligence. Fifteen—twenty minutes later you feel refreshed, awake, alive. As the day wears on and this feeling of freshness wears off, you begin to feel less efficient, more tired. Time for the early-evening period of the TM technique. The deep rest dissolves any stress accumulated during the day and the contact with creative intelligence enlivens the mind so that you are ready to engage in a full evening of enjoyable activities.

the **TM** program is fun

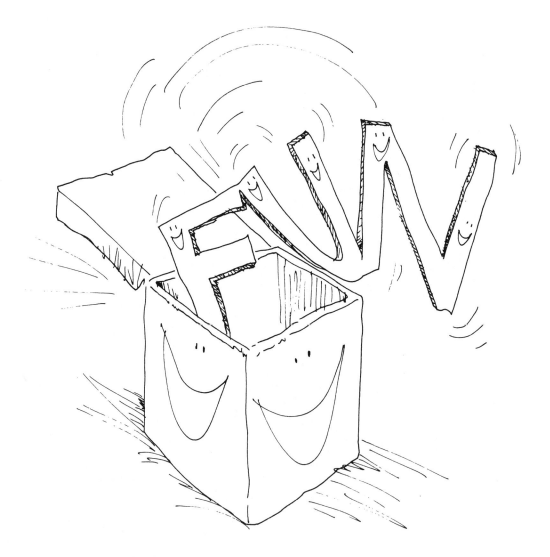

You've brought out a new concept here: one of deep rest during the Transcendental Meditation technique.

Rest is the basis of all our activity. How well we perform depends on how rested we are. When we have a good night's sleep, the activity of the day is effective and almost effortless. When we have a poor night's sleep, activity is ineffective and very difficult. When we have no rest at all, activity is all but impossible.

So we see that rest is the basis of successful activity. Successful activity leads to fulfillment, and the automatic result of fulfillment is happiness. Thus, basically, our happiness depends upon the quality of our rest. The TM technique provides a unique kind of rest that has been shown to remove deep-rooted stresses that are not normalized during sleep.

Our days are structured in cycles with a period of rest (night's sleep) and a period of activity (the day and evening). The TM program adds two additional periods of this unique style of revitalizing rest — making the entire structure of activity more flexible and enjoyable.

Levels of Rest

Physiology of Restful Alertness

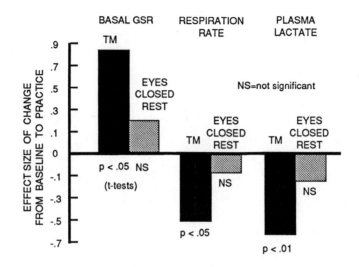

PHYSIOLOGICAL CHANGES DURING THE TM TECHNIQUE

Finding: A meta-analysis of published research on physiological changes during the TM technique — 31 studies in all — found that during meditation TM practitioners had significantly higher basal skin resistance and significantly lower respiration rates and plasma lactate levels than subjects during eyes closed rest.

Interpretation: The TM technique produces a much more profound rest than resting with the eyes closed. Increased basal skin resistance indicates a lowering of tension, while decreased respiration rate reflects greater relaxation (chart on lower breath rate). Lower plasma lactate level likewise suggests profound relaxation, since high concentrations of lactate have been associated with high anxiety and high blood pressure. These physiological changes occur spontaneously as the awareness settles to its least excited state, known as transcendental consciousness. Along with other physiological research and the subjective experience of inner wakefulness during the TM technique, these findings support the proposal that the TM technique produces a unique state of consciousness characterized by restful alertness.

References: 1. M. C. Dillbeck and D. W. Orme-Johnson, "Physiological Differences Between Transcendental Meditation and Rest," American Psychologist, in press, 1987.
2. P. Gallois, "Neurophysiological and Respiratory Changes During the Practice of Relaxation Techniques," L'encephale 10 (1984): 139-144.
3. R. Jevning, A. F. Wilson, J. P. O'Halloran, and R. N. Walsh, "Forearm blood flow and metabolism during stylized and unstylized states of decreased activation," American Journal of Physiology 245: R110-R116.
4. D. W. Orme-Johnson, "Autonomic Stability and Transcendental Meditation," Psychosomatic Medicine 35 (1973): 341-349.

As you can see in this graph, TM produces much more profound rest than ordinary relaxation, just sitting with our eyes closed.

How is TM different from sleep?

During TM the body settles to a state of very deep rest very quickly, in only a few minutes. All the various systems in the body come into a state of balance and deeply rooted stresses that sleep does not dissolve are healed. At the same time the brain functions in a more orderly, coherent way than it does when we're awake or asleep. During TM the mind is awake and alert while the body is enjoying profound rest.

The mind alert during rest? And yet the body is resting?

Right. This is a fourth state of consciousness, different from the three we already experience: deep sleep, dreaming, and waking. It is because the body is rested and the mind is still alert that we call this fourth major state of consciousness "restful alertness."

And every time someone does the TM technique they reach this state of restful alertness?

Automatically.

deep sleep consciousness

dreaming consciousness

waking consciousness

restful alertness

Greater Orderliness in Brain Functioning

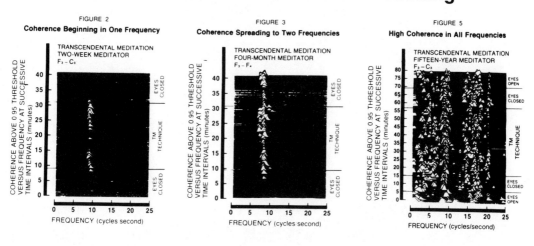

FIGURE 2
Coherence Beginning in One Frequency

FIGURE 3
Coherence Spreading to Two Frequencies

FIGURE 5
High Coherence in All Frequencies

INCREASED EEG COHERENCE

Finding: EEG coherence, as measured by a quantitative index of the degree of long range spatial ordering of the brain waves, increases between and within the cerebral hemispheres during the TM technique (ref. 1). EEG coherence increases globally among all brain areas during periods when transcendental consciousness is being subjectively experienced and the breath rate slows (ref. 2). In addition, EEG coherence increases even more during the advanced TM-Sidhi program (ref. 3) and it increases longitudinally over time as a result of the practice of the Maharishi Technology of the Unified Field (ref. 4).

Interpretation: Greater brain-wave coherence, along with the many other physiological changes produced by the TM technique, suggests a unique style of neurophysiological functioning during the practice — a unique state of restful alertness. EEG coherence has been found to be correlated with higher levels of creativity, intelligence, moral reasoning, and neuromuscular efficiency, and with experiences of higher states of consciousness. These findings support the interpretation that the increased EEG coherence produced by the TM and TM-Sidhi program indicates optimization of brain functioning. This interpretation is also consistent with research demonstrating that the practice of the Maharishi Technology of the Unified Field globally improves cognitive functioning over a wide range of measures of mental ability.

References: 1. P. Levine, "The Coherence Spectral Array (COSPAR) and its Application to the Study of Spatial Ordering in the EEG," Proceedings of the San Diego Biomedical Symposium 15 (California: 1976).
2. K. Badawi, R. K. Wallace, D. W. Orme-Johnson, and A. M. Rouzere, "Electrophysiologic Characteristics of Respiratory Suspension Periods Occurring During the Practice of the Transcendental Meditation Program," Psychosomatic Medicine 46 (1984): 267-276.
3. D. W. Orme-Johnson, G. Clements, C. T. Haynes, and K. Badaoui, "Higher States of Consciousness: EEG Coherence, Creativity, and Experiences of the Sidhis," in Scientific Research on the Transcendental Meditation Program, Collected Papers, Vol. I, ed. D. W. Orme-Johnson and J. T. Farrow (Livingston Manor, N.Y.: MERU Press, 1977), 705-712.
4. M. C. Dillbeck and E. C. Bronson, "Short-Term Longitudinal Effects of the Transcendental Meditation Technique on EEG Power and Coherence," International Journal of Neuroscience 14 (1981): 147-51.

Chapter 3

What Does the TM Program Do?

What are the benefits of the TM program?

Although we realize the body and mind are intimately connected, let us, for the sake of clarity, divide the benefits of the TM program into three categories—the mental benefits, the physical benefits, and the benefits that integrate both mind and body.

The TM program develops five fundamentals necessary for progress and success in life—Stability, Adaptability, Purification, Integration and Growth. During the course of this chapter will analyze how the Transcendental Meditation program fulfills each of these fundamentals on the level of the body (physiological), the mind (psychological), for the society as a whole (sociological), and for the environment (ecological).

Why don't you start by telling me the benefits the TM program has for the mind?

You will recall we said that rest is the basis of all our activity. This is because the clarity of our thinking depends on how rested we are. The success of our activity depends upon the quality of our thinking. Clear, direct thoughts lead spontaneously to effective, rewarding actions. Psychologists estimate that we use from 5–15% of our mental potential. This means we are only 5–15% effective—5–15% fulfilled.

If a machine functioned at only 5–15% efficiency, we would work diligently to improve it—yet many of us have had to accept limitations in our personal lives because there didn't seem to be any practical technique to improve our own mental efficiency.

During the TM technique we come into direct contact with the 85–95% of the mind we have not been using, and daily contact cultivates it—cultures it—until it is always available for our spontaneous use. The mind becomes expanded; our awareness increases.

Increased Intelligence Growth Rate

Growth of Intelligence

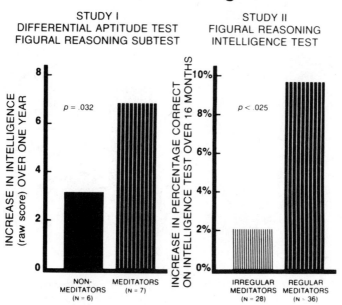

STUDY I
DIFFERENTIAL APTITUDE TEST
FIGURAL REASONING SUBTEST

STUDY II
FIGURAL REASONING
INTELLIGENCE TEST

INCREASED INTELLIGENCE GROWTH RATE

Finding: The results of an initial study showed greater increase in intelligence among meditating high school students than among non-meditating controls. These results were confirmed in a second study that indicated that a group of university students and adults who practiced the Transcendental Meditation technique regularly (N = 36) increased significantly more in intelligence than those who did not meditate regularly (N = 28) over the 16-month period after they began the Transcendental Meditation technique ($p < .025$).

Interpretation: These findings indicate that the Transcendental Meditation program increases general fluid intelligence, which enables the meditator to respond to new situations with greater adaptability, creativity, and comprehension. After the age when intelligence growth is expected to reach a plateau, meditators continue to grow in greater degrees of creative intelligence.

First Reference: André S. Tjoa, "Some Evidence That the Transcendental Meditation Program Increases Intelligence and Reduces Neuroticisim as Measured by Psychological Tests," (University of Leiden, Leiden, the Netherlands).

Second Reference: André S. Tjoa, "Meditation, Neuroticism and Intelligence: A Follow Up," Gedrag, Tijdschrift voor Psychologie 3 (the Netherlands: 1975): 167–182.

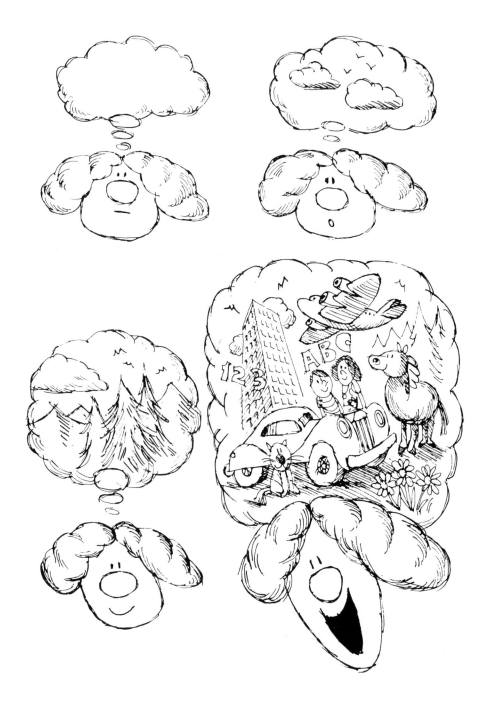

Increased Learning Ability

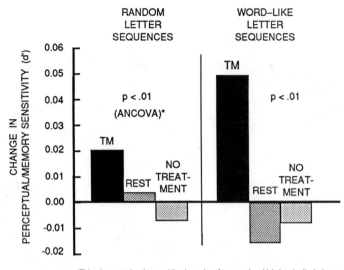

*This chart graphs the combined results of groups in which longitudinal changes were assessed between the TM technique, rest with eyes closed, and no treatment.

IMPROVED PERCEPTION AND MEMORY

Finding: College students instructed in the TM technique displayed significant improvements in performance over a two-week period on a perceptual and short-term memory test involving the identification of letter sequences presented rapidly. They were compared with subjects randomly assigned to a routine of twice-daily relaxation with eyes closed and to subjects who made no change in their daily schedule.

Interpretation: The experience of more settled and expanded states of awareness during the TM technique leads to increased effectiveness and flexibility in information processing, as reflected in improved functioning of perception and memory. The TM program has also been found to develop broader comprehension and improved ability to focus. The repeated experience of the state of restful alertness during the TM technique reduces the factors that inhibit learning, such as anxiety, and develops the mind's innate potential, bringing improved performance both at school and on the job.

References: 1. M. C. Dillbeck, "Meditation and Flexibility of Visual Perception and Verbal Problem Solving," Memory and Cognition 10 (1982): 207-15.
2. D. E. Miskiman, "Performance on a Learning Task by Subjects Who Practice the Transcendental Meditation Technique," in Scientific Research on the Transcendental Meditation Program, Collected Papers, Vol 1, ed. D. W. Orme-Johnson and J. T. Farrow (Livingston Manor, N. Y.: MERU Press, 1977): 382-84.

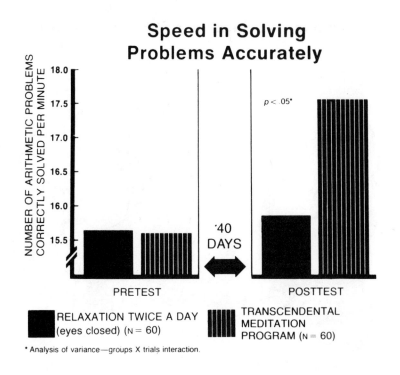

Speed in Solving Problems Accurately

NUMBER OF ARITHMETIC PROBLEMS CORRECTLY SOLVED PER MINUTE

$p < .05^*$

·40 DAYS

PRETEST   POSTTEST

RELAXATION TWICE A DAY (eyes closed) (N = 60)

TRANSCENDENTAL MEDITATION PROGRAM (N = 60)

* Analysis of variance—groups X trials interaction.

INCREASED ORDERLINESS OF THINKING

Finding: After beginning the practice of the Transcendental Meditation technique, meditators significantly increased their speed in solving arithmetic problems accurately. Two facts were found:

1. The efficiency of solving arithmetic problems increased in meditators who practiced the TM technique 20 minutes twice daily, compared with members of a control group who relaxed for an equivalent period of time twice daily.

2. A separate test of memory showed that improved organization of memory continued to stabilize even while the meditators were engaged in problem solving.

Interpretation: These results show that the Transcendental Meditation program increases the clarity and efficiency of conscious thought processes and at the same time improves the unconscious processes, leading to spontaneous and purposeful organization of thought. More orderly, purposeful, intelligent thought indicates unfoldment of full mental potential.

Reference: Donald E. Miskiman, "The Effect of the Transcendental Meditation Program on the Organization of Thinking and Recall (Secondary Organization)," (University of Alberta, Edmonton, Alberta, Canada).

Change in Academic Performance

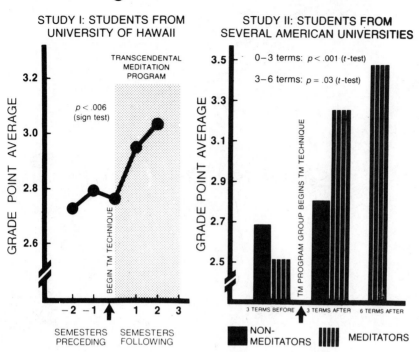

STUDY I: STUDENTS FROM
UNIVERSITY OF HAWAII

STUDY II: STUDENTS FROM
SEVERAL AMERICAN UNIVERSITIES

GRADE POINT AVERAGE

TRANSCENDENTAL
MEDITATION
PROGRAM

$p < .006$
(sign test)

BEGIN TM TECHNIQUE

SEMESTERS
PRECEDING

SEMESTERS
FOLLOWING

0–3 terms: $p < .001$ (t-test)

3–6 terms: $p = .03$ (t-test)

TM PROGRAM GROUP BEGINS TM TECHNIQUE

3 TERMS BEFORE   3 TERMS AFTER   6 TERMS AFTER

NON-
MEDITATORS

MEDITATORS

IMPROVED ACADEMIC PERFORMANCE
UNIVERSITY STUDENTS

Finding: In two studies academic performance, as measured by grade point average (GPA), was shown to improve sharply after students began the Transcendental Meditation technique. Study I is a retrospective study of students at the University of Hawaii. The GPA for a minimum of two semesters before the students began the TM program was compared to their GPA for a minimum of one semester after they began the programme. Study II is a retrospective study comparing meditators with a matched control group of non-meditators.

Interpretation: The generalized improvement in neurophysiological and psychological functioning caused by the Transcendental Meditation technique naturally brings about improvement in a holistic measure of mental effectiveness, the ability to succeed in academic studies. Thus, the TM program is found to bring about a systematic development of creative intelligence.

First Reference: Study I: Roy W. Collier, "The Effect of Transcendental Meditation upon University Academic Attainment," (Paper presented at the Pacific Northwest Conference on Foreign Languages, Seattle, Washington, U.S.A.).

Second Reference: Study II: Dennis P. Heaton and David W. Orme-Johnson, "The Transcendental Meditation Program and Academic Achievement," (Maharishi International University, Fairfield, Iowa, U.S.A).

71

You mean students can get better grades if they start the TM program?

Yes, that's been the experience. Thousands and thousands of students have found that they get better grades, enjoy school more, and have time left over for their friends.

And for those not in school?

Job performance improves.

Increased Productivity I

Change in Productivity

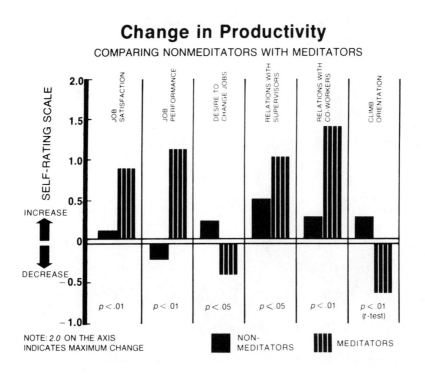

COMPARING NONMEDITATORS WITH MEDITATORS

NOTE: 2.0 ON THE AXIS
INDICATES MAXIMUM CHANGE

NON-MEDITATORS   MEDITATORS

INCREASED PRODUCTIVITY I

Finding: In this study 42 students practicing the Transcendental Meditation technique an average of 11 months showed more job satisfaction, better job performance, more stability in their jobs, and better interpersonal relationships with their supervisors and co-workers than members of a control group. Whereas meditators reported that they felt less anxiety about promotion (shown by reduced climb orientation), their fellow employees saw them as moving ahead quickly.

Interpretation: At every level of organization performance improves when the members practice the Transcendental Meditation technique. Within the organizational structure meditators succeed more quickly and experience less anxiety. This indicates that a faster pace of progress is natural for persons practicing the TM technique.

Reference: David R. Frew, "Transcendental Meditation and Productivity," *Academy of Management Journal* 17, no. 2 (U.S.A.: 1974): 362–368.

Change in Productivity

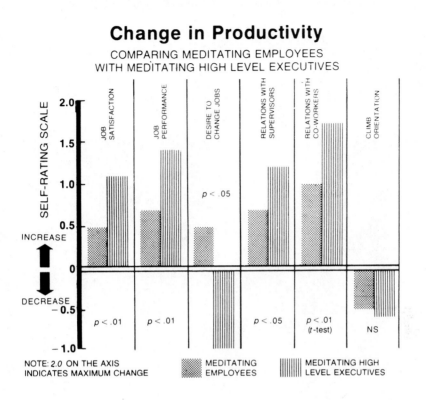

COMPARING MEDITATING EMPLOYEES
WITH MEDITATING HIGH LEVEL EXECUTIVES

NOTE: 2.0 ON THE AXIS
INDICATES MAXIMUM CHANGE

MEDITATING EMPLOYEES

MEDITATING HIGH LEVEL EXECUTIVES

INCREASED PRODUCTIVITY II

Finding: Executives at higher levels of responsibility who practice the TM technique showed improved job performance, more job satisfaction, more stability in their jobs, and improved interpersonal relationships when compared with meditators at lower levels of organization.

Interpretation: The higher the individual's level of authority, the greater is the gain in productivity through the Transcendental Meditation program. The study indicates that although individuals at all levels of an organization gain in productivity through the Transcendental Meditation program, those at more responsible levels, where greater productivity is needed, find an even greater application for the increased creative intelligence systematically developed through the TM program.

Reference: David R. Frew, "Transcendental Meditation and Productivity," *Academy of Management Journal 17, no. 2* (U.S.A.: 1974): 362–368.

Change in Job Performance

COMPARING (1) NONMEDITATORS WITH MEDITATORS,
(2) MEDITATING EMPLOYEES WITH MEDITATING
HIGH LEVEL EXECUTIVES

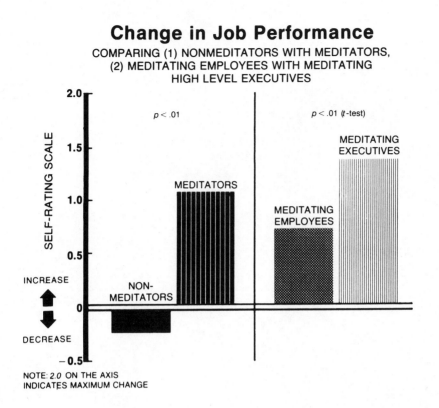

IMPROVED JOB PERFORMANCE

Finding: At all levels of organization those who practice the TM technique showed a significant increase in job performance compared with non-meditating controls. Meditating executives at higher levels of responsibility showed a comparatively greater increase in performance than those at less responsible levels.

Interpretation: Individuals at all levels of organization benefit from the development of creative intelligence through practice of the Transcendental Meditation technique. Executives at higher levels of responsibility, where greater creativity is demanded, find an even greater application for increased creative intelligence.

Reference: David R. Frew, "Transcendental Meditation and Productivity," *Academy of Management Journal 17, no. 2* (U.S.A.: 1974): 362–368.

And job satisfaction, too!

Increased Job Satisfaction

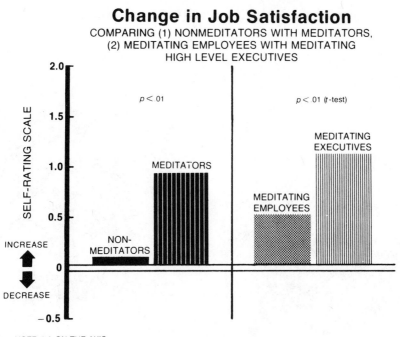

Change in Job Satisfaction
COMPARING (1) NONMEDITATORS WITH MEDITATORS,
(2) MEDITATING EMPLOYEES WITH MEDITATING
HIGH LEVEL EXECUTIVES

NOTE: *2.0* ON THE AXIS
INDICATES MAXIMUM CHANGE

INCREASED JOB SATISFACTION

Finding: Forty-two subjects practicing the Transcendental Meditation technique an average of 11 months showed a greater increase in job satisfaction than did non-meditators over the same period of time. Executives at higher levels of management showed the greatest increase.

Interpretation: Because the Transcendental Meditation program improves job performance and thus increases the success of individuals at all levels of an organization, it brings increased job satisfaction.

Reference: David R. Frew, "Transcendental Meditation and Productivity," *Academy of Management Journal* 17, no. 2 (U.S.A.: 1974): 362–368.

Improved Relations with Supervisors

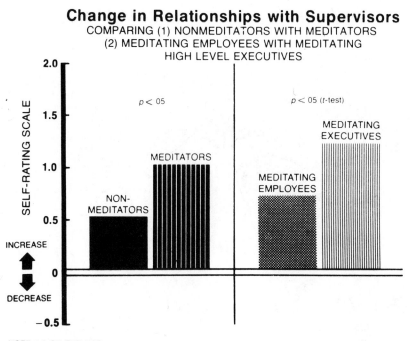

Change in Relationships with Supervisors
COMPARING (1) NONMEDITATORS WITH MEDITATORS
(2) MEDITATING EMPLOYEES WITH MEDITATING HIGH LEVEL EXECUTIVES

SELF-RATING SCALE

2.0

1.5 $p < 05$ $p < 05$ (t-test)

1.0

0.5

INCREASE

0

DECREASE

−0.5

MEDITATORS

NON-MEDITATORS

MEDITATING EMPLOYEES

MEDITATING EXECUTIVES

NOTE: *2.0* ON THE AXIS
INDICATES MAXIMUM CHANGE

IMPROVED RELATIONSHIPS WITH SUPERVISORS

Finding: This study showed that the Transcendental Meditation program was effective in significantly improving employees' working relationships with their supervisors. Improvement was found to be comparatively greater for those at higher levels of organization.

Interpretation: The Transcendental Meditation program leads to more rewarding and productive interpersonal relationships in business by improving each individual's ability to do his job effectively and amiably while simultaneously increasing his stability and warmth of personality.

Reference: David R. Frew, "Transcendental Meditation and Productivity," *Academy of Management Journal* 17, no. 2 (U.S.A.: 1974): 362–368.

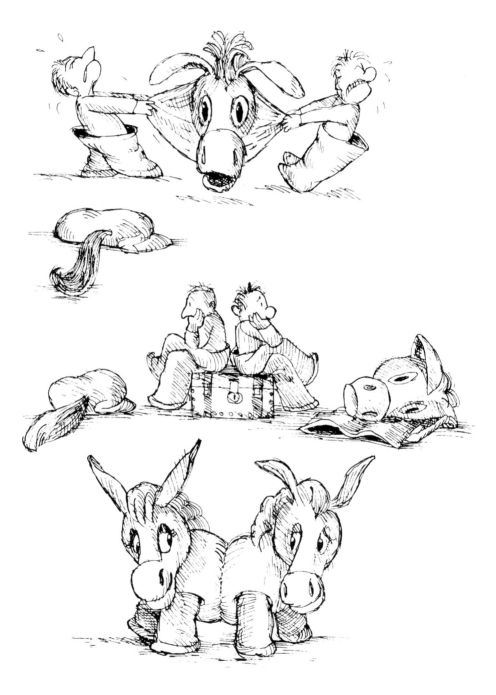

Change in Relationships with Co-Workers
COMPARING (1) NONMEDITATORS WITH MEDITATORS, (2) MEDITATING EMPLOYEES WITH MEDITATING HIGH LEVEL EXECUTIVES

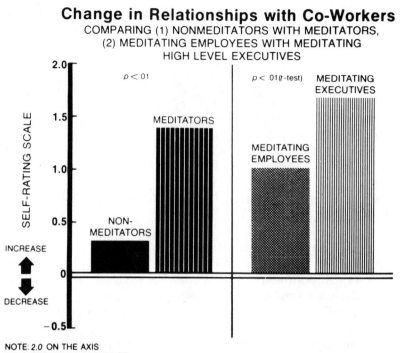

NOTE: *2.0* ON THE AXIS
INDICATES MAXIMUM CHANGE

IMPROVED RELATIONSHIPS WITH CO-WORKERS

Finding: This study showed that working relationships with co-workers were significantly improved through practice of the Transcendental Meditation technique. This improvement was seen at both employee and executive levels.

Interpretation: This study shows that the Transcendental Meditation program brings about improved relationships at all levels of organization, indicating more harmonious interaction among different individuals working together within an organization. This may be seen as the sociological consequence of the effect of the Transcendental Meditation program on the individual—development of broadened awareness along with the ability of focus.

Reference: David R. Frew, "Transcendental Meditation and Productivity," *Academy of Management Journal* 17, no. 2 (U.S.A.: 1974): 362–368.

What is happening is really quite simple. Intelligence increases as a result of the TM program, therefore the ability to do *anything* improves.

But won't we all turn out the same? That would be dull!

No, not the same. The key word is *potential*. We each have a different potential, that is, different talents and abilities. The tragedy is that we have developed only a small portion of that potential. This extends to specific potential as well. We do not all end up with the same ability. Some will find calculus a breeze. Others will have no difficulty writing epic poems before breakfast.

The TM program brings a revolutionary concept into psychology—the fact that it is possible to greatly increase intelligence and creativity in adults. Now it is actually possible to become more intelligent as we acquire the experience of living.

With the TM technique our thinking becomes more flexible, more lively. After beginning the TM program, time ceases to be an enemy and becomes a friend. Before we started the program we thought, "Before long, I'll be five years older." But after starting the TM program we say, "In five years I'll have been practicing the TM technique five years longer." And we know that five years of the TM program means five years of increasing intelligence, expanding awareness, and growing stability.

So rather than becoming more and more the same, meditators become more and more different?

A useful analogy might be an orchard of trees, their roots deep in the same earth, yet their branches each yielding different fruit. We become more grounded in our common basis of creative intelligence, yet our expressions of that creative intelligence become stronger and more independent. And interestingly enough, that increased independence and individuality is enjoyed along with more and more harmony with others and with the environment.

Now let's go on to the physical benefits of the TM program.

The key word in discussing the TM program benefits to the body is *rest*. The body automatically heals and rejuvenates itself when allowed to rest. We experience this at night when we sleep: much of the tension and fatigue of the day is dissolved by that rest.

So if the body is rested during a night's sleep, why do we need the TM technique?

Although nightly sleep dissolves some fatigue and stress, the degree of rest is not complete enough to remove more deeply rooted stresses. To remove these stresses we need the deeper rest of the TM technique. This deeper rest twice daily also improves health, strengthens the body, and produces greater flexibility.

How can something be strong *and* flexible at the same time?

When speaking of the body, flexibility *means* strength. It's the old story of the willow and the oak tree. The willow bends to the strong wind, the oak tree tries to remain immovable. After the storm, the willow, flexible, stands; the oak, inflexible, has fallen.

Man has survived as the crown of physical creation because of his flexibility. A species survives if it can adapt to changing environmental conditions.

Life is full of change, jolts and sensations. If we are rigid, if we are not flexible, then these impulses can become intolerable bombardments, overloads to the system.

But if we can adapt to these experiences, they become part of the play of life.

This brings us to one of the Fundamentals of Progress, Adaptability.

ADAPTABILITY

PHYSIOLOGICAL ADAPTABILITY

The TRANSCENDENTAL MEDITATION technique provides coherent rest to the nervous system, as indicated by:

> relaxation of the entire system:
>> marked reduction in oxygen consumption
>> natural change in breath rate and volume
>> natural change in heart rate
>> increased balance of autonomic nervous system
>
> biochemical indication of relaxation
> electrophysiological changes indicating relaxation
>
> electroencephalographic changes indicating relaxation, as well as increased stability, orderliness, and coherence of brain activity

The daily cycle of deep rest provided by the alternation of the TRANSCENDENTAL MEDITATION technique and regular activity develops physiological adaptability—the ability of the nervous system to adjust to change with minimum consumption of energy—as indicated by: rapid recovery from stressful situations such as loud noises, exertion, sleep deprivation, and by increased vital capacity, increased cardiovascular efficiency, increased ease of breathing, normalization of weight, and improved athletic performance.

Furthermore, the greater adaptability through the TRANSCENDENTAL MEDITATION technique is indicated by: improved resistance to disease, less susceptibility to bronchial asthma, high blood pressure and insomnia.

These physiological changes account for the psychological changes.

PSYCHOLOGICAL ADAPTABILITY

Through the practice of the TRANSCENDENTAL MEDITATION technique, psychological adaptability—the ability of the mind to adjust to change for survival and progress—increases, as indicated by:

increased intelligence

broader comprehension and improved ability to focus attention

increased perceptual ability

increased learning ability

faster reactions

superior perceptual-motor performance

improved academic performance

increased self-sufficiency

improved organization of memory

increased speed in solving problems accurately

increased innovation

increased energy level

increased creativity

The TRANSCENDENTAL MEDITATION technique expands the conscious capacity of the mind through the experience of "profound wakefulness," "pure consciousness," or "unbounded awareness." An integrated, expanded consciousness is capable of broad vision and can at once intuit a more comprehensive range of any situation—the mind's adaptability increases in the service of existence and evolution.

These physiological and psychological changes account for the sociological changes.

SOCIOLOGICAL ADAPTABILITY

Through the TRANSCENDENTAL MEDITATION program, sociological adaptability—the ability of the members of society to change for maximum mutual benefit—increases, as indicated by:

more rewarding and productive interpersonal relationships in business

increased capacity for intimate contact

increased sociability

increased respect

flexibility in the application of one's own values

decreased rigidity

reduced social inadequacy

reduced social introversion

reduced antisocial behavior

reduced irritability

reduced use of alcohol and cigarettes

reduced use of nonprescribed drugs

reduced anxiety

increased tolerance

increased cordiality and good humor

These physiological, psychological, and sociological changes account for the ecological changes.

ECOLOGICAL ADAPTABILITY

It is our common experience that the homes of meditators are found to be more cordial, soothing, and harmonious, and in the homes of those nonmeditators where conflicts and dissension prevail, guests cannot avoid experiencing that discordant atmosphere.

Travelers likewise have experienced that their feelings change as they pass by certain villages. This is due to the quality of life in the village. For the same reason, international travelers have experienced that different countries project different feelings and this is clearly noticeable even while crossing the national borders.

From these common experiences it is obvious that the ecosphere shows a great range of adaptability and automatically adjusts to the influence created by man. It is fortunate for us who are concerned with the problems of ecology today that the scientific research on the TRAN-SCENDENTAL MEDITATION program has shown that life-supporting values increase in the meditator's physiology, psychology, and social life, as indicated by the scientific charts. These findings satisfy man's current search for an effective means to save and enrich the ecology because they show that the TRANSCENDENTAL MEDITATION program is the one thing that every man can do to produce life-supporting influences in his environment and radiate the influence of harmony in the ecosphere. The positive influence generated by the meditator enlivens and enriches the life-supporting quality of the ecosphere, thereby freeing it from the stress of negative influences, enabling it to be more refined and generous, and therefore more adaptable.

Isn't adaptability also a function of the mind?

Definitely. Expansion of the mind and flexibility of the body create true adaptability.

Can't we be too adaptable?

Stability is essential as well. An autumn leaf, drifting with the wind, is very adaptable––it goes wherever the wind sends it. Stability insures the fact that from one day to the next we continue to express the values we cherish and to uphold the responsibilities we have undertaken.

Stability is most certainly a Fundamental of Progress.

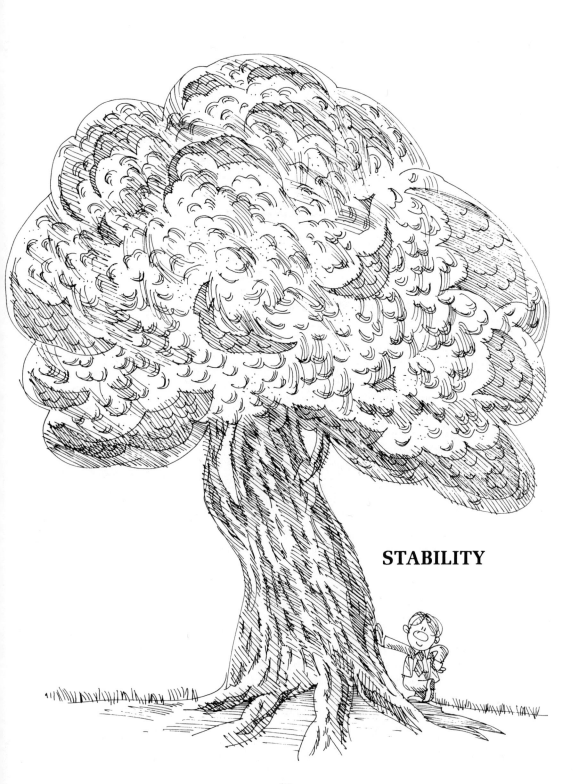

STABILITY

PHYSIOLOGICAL STABILITY

Through the practice of the TRANSCENDENTAL MEDITATION technique, physiological stability—the stable functioning of physiological processes—increases, as indicated by:

stable state of rest:
    metabolic stability
    biochemical stability
    electrophysiological stability

stabilization of brain rhythms

interhemispheric balance of brain activity

habituation of stable, orderly brain functioning in activity

improved physiology stabilized in activity:
    increased cardiovascular efficiency
    increased vital capacity
    increased respiratory efficiency
    increased metabolic stability

rapid recovery of a stable physiological baseline:
    improved recovery from exertion
    increased autonomic stability
    more effective interaction with the environment

stabilized health:
    improved resistance to disease
    faster recovery from sleep deprivation
    normalization of high blood pressure
    relief from insomnia
    beneficial effects on bronchial asthma
    reduced use of alcohol and cigarettes
    reduced use of nonprescribed drugs
    normalization of weight

These physiological changes account for the psychological changes.

PSYCHOLOGICAL STABILITY

Through the practice of the TRANSCENDENTAL MEDITATION technique, psychological stability—maintenance of mental and emotional balance—increases, as indicated by:

increased emotional stability

decreased anxiety

reduced depression

reduced neuroticism

stronger intellect

stability of attention

increased inner control

increased self-confidence

stabilization of organized memory

increased individuality

increased self-actualization

increased self-esteem

Psychological stability develops automatically when the mind repeatedly gains and becomes habituated to its most stable status—pure consciousness—through the regular practice of the TRANSCENDENTAL MEDITATION technique. The mind and emotions become balanced through the experience of pure consciousness, resulting in purposeful thought and action, which stabilize the entire psychology.

These physiological and psychological changes account for the sociological changes.

SOCIOLOGICAL STABILITY

Through the practice of the TRANSCENDENTAL MEDITATION technique, sociological stability—stability of interpersonal relations—increases, as indicated by:

improved relations between co-workers and supervisors

growing stabilizing influences:
    increased respect
    increased cordiality
    increased sociability
    increased good humor
    increased tolerance
    increased tendency to see man as essentially good
    increased job stability

decreased disruptive influences:
    decreased social inadequacy
    decreased irritability
    reduced use of nonprescribed drugs
    stabilization of unstable members of society—more effective rehabilitation

improved quality of city life—decreased crime rate

developed capacity for warm interpersonal relationships

These physiological, psychological, and sociological changes account for the ecological changes.

ECOLOGICAL STABILITY

Through the practice of the TRANSCENDENTAL MEDITATION technique, the meditator grows in physiological, psychological, and sociological stability. As man is the most influential member of the environment, when he grows in stability, naturally he radiates the influence of stability around him, securing balance and intensifying harmony in the environment. This is how the TRANSCENDENTAL MEDITATION program is a direct means of promoting ecological stability.

increased physiological stability:
    increased stability of the autonomic nervous system
    stable state of rest
    improved physiology stabilized
    stabilized health

increased psychological stability:
    increased emotional stability
    increased inner control
    increased self-regard and self-confidence
    decreased anxiety
    decreased depression
    decreased neuroticism

increased sociological stability:
    increased job stability
    stability of interpersonal relationships
    reduced use of alcohol and cigarettes
    reduced use of nonprescribed drugs
    reduced crime rate
    more effective rehabilitation

The TM program makes the nervous system more stable.

Spontaneous
Skin Resistance Responses

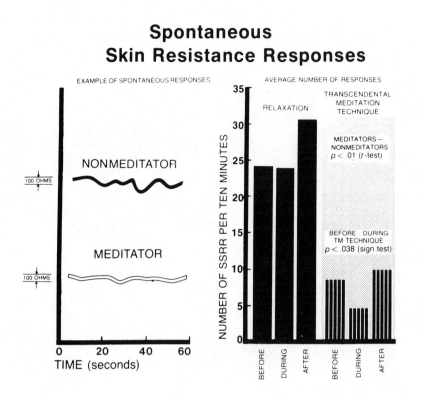

INCREASED AUTONOMIC STABILITY

Finding: Subjects practicing the Transcendental Meditation technique were found to have fewer spontaneous skin resistance responses (SSRR) than non-meditating control subjects ($p < .01$), indicating greater stability in the autonomic nervous system.

Interpretation: The Transcendental Meditation technique stabilizes the nervous system, as shown by fewer spontaneous skin resistance responses. This stability continues to be maintained after practice of the technique. Psychophysiologists have generally shown that a condition of fewer skin resistance responses is highly correlated with greater resistance to environmental stress, psychosomatic disease, and behavioral instability, as well as with greater efficiency in the activity of the nervous system. The Transcendental Meditation technique reduces the 'noise level' of the nervous system and thereby frees more energy for perception, thought, and purposeful activity.

Reference: David W. Orme-Johnson, "Autonomic Stability and Transcendental Meditation," *Psychosomatic Medicine* 35, no. 4 (U.S.A.: 1973): 341–349.

The TM program also improves adaptability and makes us more accurate and flexible in our response to the environment.

Faster Reaction Time

Change in Reaction Time

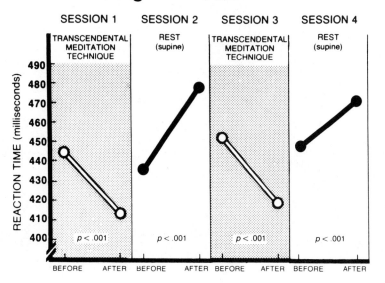

FASTER REACTIONS

Finding: Twenty-five subjects were measured over four different sessions of either practicing the Transcendental Meditation technique or relaxing. The Transcendental Meditation technique was consistently found to speed up reactions, whereas resting in a supine position resulted in a slowing of reactions.

Interpretation: The Transcendental Meditation technique speeds up reactions, indicating increased alertness, improved coordination of mind and body, and improved efficiency in perception and performance. This experiment also shows that the TM technique results in significantly more freshness and alertness than is achieved by merely lying down. The state produced by the TM technique is a superior form of coherent deep rest.

First Reference: David W. Orme-Johnson, David Kolb, and J. Russell Hebert, "An Experimental Analysis of the Effects of the Transcendental Meditation Technique on Reaction Time" (Maharishi International University, Fairfield, Iowa, U.S.A.).

Second Reference: Robert Shaw and David Kolb, "Reaction Time Following the Transcendental Meditation Technique," (University of Texas at Austin, Austin, Texas, U.S.A.).

Third Reference: Stuart Appelle and Lawrence Oswald, "Simple Reaction Time as a Function of Alertness and Prior Mental Activity," *Perceptual and Motor Skills 38* (U.S.A.: 1974): 1263–1268.

Superior Perceptual-Motor Performance

Mirror Star-Tracing Test

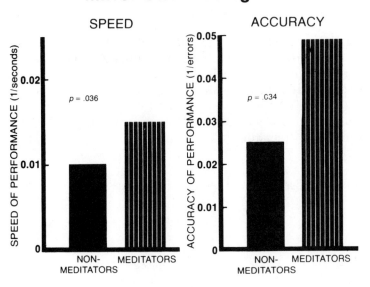

SUPERIOR PERCEPTUAL-MOTOR PERFORMANCE

Finding: Subjects who practice the Transcendental Meditation technique performed faster and more accurately on a complex perceptual-motor test (Mirror Star-Tracing Test). The test measures the ability to trace a pattern while watching its reflection in a mirror without becoming disoriented.

Interpretation: Performance as measured by this test is relevant to such tasks as driving a car, hitting a target, and performing in many different sports. The superior performance of meditators indicates that the Transcendental Meditation program produces greater coordination between mind and body, greater flexibility, increased perceptual awareness, superior resistance to disorientation, greater efficiency, and improved neuromuscular integration.

Reference: Karen S. Blasdell, "The Effects of the Transcendental Meditation Technique upon a Complex Perceptual-Motor Task," (University of California, Los Angeles, California, U.S.A.).

You mentioned health?

The first thing the doctor says when he learns of illness is "Get plenty of rest." This is because he knows the body's natural healing and rejuvenating qualities are most active when the body is at rest. The TM technique provides the body with an excellent basis for health because it provides even deeper rest than sleep. The word "disease" is significant. It means dis-ease—a lack of ease. TM provides the body with unbounded ease—twice a day. This removes the cause of physical ill health.

We know that heart disease is the number one cause of death in the United States.

Change in Heart Rate

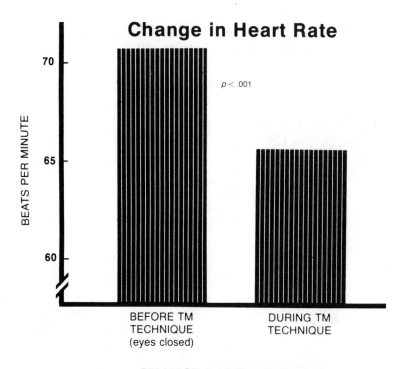

CHANGE IN HEART RATE

Finding: Heart rate was recorded by electrocardiogram in 11 long-term meditators (average time meditating 25 months, average age 23 years). During the Transcendental Meditation technique the average decrease in heart rate was five beats per minute compared with the rate before practice of the technique (sitting with eyes closed).

Interpretation: When taken together with additional data from the same study, this finding suggests that cardiac output also decreases, implying a reduction in the work load of the heart during the Transcendental Meditation technique.

Reference: Robert Keith Wallace, "The Physiological Effects of Transcendental Meditation: A Proposed Fourth Major State of Consciousness," (Ph.D. Thesis, Department of Physiology, University of California, Los Angeles, California, U.S.A., 1970).

This chart shows that the heart rate decreases during the TM technique. This means that the TM program gives the heart a significant rest—twice daily.

Also, the TM program normalizes blood pressure.

117

Normalization of High Blood Pressure:
Reduced Hypertension

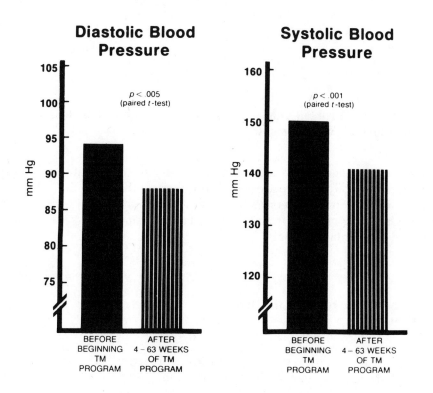

Diastolic Blood Pressure

p < .005
(paired *t*-test)

mm Hg

BEFORE BEGINNING TM PROGRAM — AFTER 4 – 63 WEEKS OF TM PROGRAM

Systolic Blood Pressure

p < .001
(paired *t*-test)

mm Hg

BEFORE BEGINNING TM PROGRAM — AFTER 4 – 63 WEEKS OF TM PROGRAM

NORMALIZATION OF HIGH BLOOD PRESSURE

Finding: Systolic and diastolic arterial blood pressures were recorded 1,119 times in 22 hypertensive patients before and after they began the Transcendental Meditation program. The decreases in blood pressure after patients began practicing the Transcendental Meditation technique were statistically significant.

Interpretation: These findings indicate that the Transcendental Meditation program is useful and effective as an adjunct in the treatment of high blood pressure. In the U.S.A. alone essential hypertension affects over 23 million citizens, including one out of every three adult males. High blood pressure increases the risk of disease and death due to heart attack, stroke, and damage to vital organs. Autonomic liability (instability) has been shown to be a precursor to hypertension. The Transcendental Meditation program promotes autonomic stability and may be important in both the treatment of hypertension and the prevention of cardiovascular disease. Note: People under the care of a physician should go by their physician's advice in coordinating participation in the TM program with ongoing medical care and medication.

First Reference: Herbert Benson and Robert Keith Wallace, "Decreased Blood Pressure in Hypertensive Subjects Who Practiced Meditation," Supplement II to *Circulation* 45 and 46 (U.S.A.: 1972).

Second Reference: Barry Blackwell, Irwin Hanenson, Saul Bloomfield, Herbert Magenheim, Sanford Nidich, and Peter Gartside, "Effects of Transcendental Meditation on Blood Pressure: A Controlled Pilot Experiment," *Journal of Psychosomatic Medicine* 37, (U.S.A.: 1975): 86.

If the TM program could reduce the incidence of cardiovascular disease—heart attack, stroke—and nothing more, its benefits would be overwhelming.

Aren't many heart problems caused, or at least complicated, by worry—and isn't worry mental, not physical?

Yes, and yes. Here again we reach an impasse in trying to separate the activity of the mind and body. Not only does the mind affect the "obvious" physical ailments—heart trouble, ulcers, asthma, psychosomatic illnesses—but medical authorities estimate that from 60–90% of *all* physical illness is caused or aggravated by mental tension.

The TM technique removes this tension from the mind?

The "tension" is actually in the body in the form of "stress." The quality of our thinking is directly influenced by the condition of the body. If the body is rested and at ease, the mind is relaxed and effective. If the body is tired and stressed, the mind is worried and tense.

It's another of those vicious circles: the more stress we have, the more we get.

Yes, and it works both ways. Not only does the TM program remove the stress that is in the body, it also prevents new stress from building up. And the less stress we have, the less stress we get. A clear mind perceives situations more fully, and the more we see, the less upsetting life is.

How does that work?

I'm sure at one time or another we've walked into a dark room and—even if it was in our own home—experienced fear. Yet, as soon as the light was turned on we could see that everything was all right. As our awareness expanded to include the whole room, our fear vanished.

Many of the situations we perceive as stressful are merely a reflection of our own limited perception—our own narrowness of vision.

What do you mean by "stress"?

Stress is any chemical or physical abnormality in the body, in the nervous system. It is caused by overload. When some physical or emotional pressure of experience distorts the system, that overload is stress. When the stresses are too deeply rooted or too numerous to be relieved by a good night's sleep, then they accumulate and we become increasingly ineffective in our activity.

Then stress must interfere with everything we do!

Yes, but consider the consequences of eliminating stress stored in the nervous system. When we're stressed, we see things negatively; when we're refreshed and rested, we perceive positively. When the nervous system is strained and tired, our activity seems fruitless and futile; when our mind is clear and alert, we can make the best use of everything around us without even trying.

When we're hassled and upset, the tiniest irritation can make it impossible to communicate. How many times have you felt that if a situation didn't upset you so much, it would be *easy* to do the right thing?

More than I care to remember.

This is because stress keeps building up in our lives and overshadows the normal, easy enjoyment of life that we *should* be experiencing. When stresses are dissolved by the deep rest of the TM technique, the nervous system is allowed to function in a holistic and balanced way. Then all our thoughts and actions are creative and successful. And all of our relationships are natural and rewarding.

Will the TM program remove everybody's inhibitions?

If by inhibitions you mean obstacles that keep us from functioning freely, then you're talking about stress. The TM program will definitely eliminate stress.

But aren't some inhibitions good?

Manners are good. Inhibitions are not good. Inhibitions are involuntary. We have no *choice*. They are imprisoning. Good manners are a matter of choice. We follow certain impulses and don't follow others. Right and moral action is the natural result of a stress-free nervous system.

So these stresses distort perception and inhibit expression.

Yes.

Change in Auditory Discrimination

INCREASED PERCEPTUAL ABILITY

Finding: The ability of meditators to discriminate small differences in the length of auditory tones was significantly better ($p<.02$) after practicing the Transcendental Meditation technique than after simply sitting with eyes closed. Experimental group A relaxed with eyes closed first, then meditated. Experimental group B meditated, then relaxed with eyes closed. In both cases performance immediately following the Transcendental Meditation technique was superior to that immediately following relaxation.

Interpretation: This indicates an increased refinement of perception following the TM technique and suggests that the deep rest produced by the technique reduces the 'noise' in the perceptual system, resulting in improved information-processing capabilities. This conclusion is supported by the finding that reactions are also faster after the Transcendental Meditation technique than after simply lying down with eyes closed. The Transcendental Meditation technique improves the 'signal-to-noise' ratio of the nervous system, resulting in more sensitive perceptions.

Reference: Michael Pirot, "The Effects of the Transcendental Meditation Technique upon Auditory Discrimination," (University of Victoria, Victoria, British Columbia, Canada).

As the regular practice of the Transcendental Meditation technique continues, we notice an increasing sense of freedom. Our thoughts and feelings are more freely and clearly expressed. This process of releasing stress and tension in a totally effortless way brings us to another Fundamental of Progress fulfilled by the TM program, Purification.

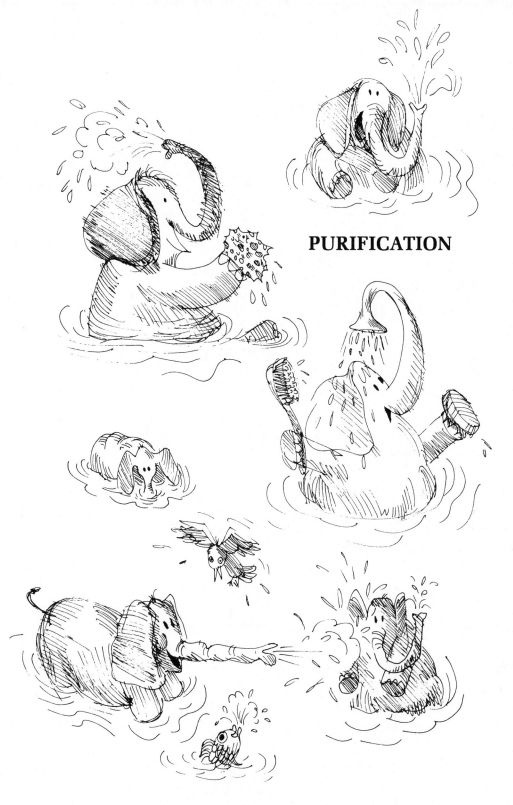

PURIFICATION

PHYSIOLOGICAL PURIFICATION

Through the practice of the TRANSCENDENTAL MEDITATION technique, physiological purification—the normalization of the physiology—increases, as indicated by:

> increased efficiency of the body's natural processes of purification by providing a deep state of rest:
>> metabolic rest
>>
>> natural change in breath rate and volume
>>
>> natural change in heart rate
>>
>> increased balance of sympathetic (active) and parasympathetic (restful) aspects of the nervous system
>>
>> biochemical indications of relaxation
>>
>> electrophysiological indications of relaxation
>>
>> electroencephalographic changes indicating relaxation
>
> increased efficiency of the purifying processes of sleeping and dreaming:
>> faster recovery from sleep deprivation
>>
>> reduced insomnia
>
> normalization of the autonomic nervous system—greater stability
>
> biochemical purification
>
> normalization of high blood pressure
>
> beneficial effects on bronchial asthma
>
> improved resistance to disease
>
> normalization of weight

The TRANSCENDENTAL MEDITATION technique produces such profound rest that it dissolves deep-rooted stresses that are not eliminated by the ordinary rest of sleep. This physiological purification stabilizes normal health and helps prevent disease.

These physiological changes account for the psychological changes.

PSYCHOLOGICAL PURIFICATION

Through the practice of the TRANSCENDENTAL MEDITATION technique, psychological purification—reduction of negativity and increased positivity in thinking, understanding, and emotions—increases, as indicated by:

increased positive qualities:
- increased emotional stability
- increased spontaneity
- increased self-actualization
- increased self-confidence and naturalness
- increased self-esteem
- increased innovation
- increased individuality
- increased tolerance
- increased positive behavior
- increased intelligence
- increased orderliness of thinking

reduced negative traits:
- decreased anxiety
- decreased depression
- decreased personal inadequacy and rigidity
- decreased neurosis

The TRANSCENDENTAL MEDITATION program does not directly concern itself with problems or negativity of any kind. The technique allows the mind to effortlessly experience pure consciousness, the supreme value of psychological purification. As pure consciousness is the basis of all progress and as this is brought about by the process of physiological and psychological purification, it is obvious that purification is essential to progress—a natural means of purification is invariably a natural means to progress.

These physiological and psychological changes account for the sociological changes.

SOCIOLOGICAL PURIFICATION

Through the practice of the TRANSCENDENTAL MEDITATION technique, sociological purification—the reduction of negativity in society—increases, as indicated by:

decreased crime rate

decreased antisocial tendencies resulting in more effective rehabilitation

decreased use of nonprescribed drugs

reduced use of alcohol and cigarettes

increased sociability

increased tolerance

increased good humor

increased cordiality

increased tendency to view man as essentially good

developed capacity for warm interpersonal relationships

broadened comprehension

increased comprehension of the consequences of one's behavior

Considering the phenomenon of sociological purification objectively, as members of society rise to more comprehensive awareness through the physiological and psychological purification brought about by the TRANSCENDENTAL MEDITATION program, the institutions of social purification, such as law enforcement agencies and the judiciary, prisons and rehabilitation centers, educational systems, and hospitals spontaneously fulfill their objectives. The activities of these organizations will become more effective as their members rise to full potential.

These physiological, psychological, and sociological changes account for the ecological changes.

ECOLOGICAL PURIFICATION

Through the TRANSCENDENTAL MEDITATION program, ecological purification increases—wholeness of ecological values blossoms—harmony becomes more and more evident
in the midst of diversity. This is on the basis of the total effect of the practice resulting in:

reduced negativity

more harmonious interaction with the environment

Considering the phenomenon of ecological purification objectively, mechanisms of self-purifi-
cation are found in the ecosystem (e.g., decomposers and scavengers) as in the individual (e.g.,
the immune system—the body's ability to resist disease). These intrinsic purifying mechanisms
and their balance in nature can be overwhelmed by the negative influence that man may
produce due to his lack of total vision, his short-sightedness and selfishness, and even by the
undue aggression coming from his stressed life. The TRANSCENDENTAL MEDITATION
program, developing fullness in man, has the ability to promote life-supporting influences and
thereby naturally maintain ecological purification, eliminating the very basis of all pollution.

131

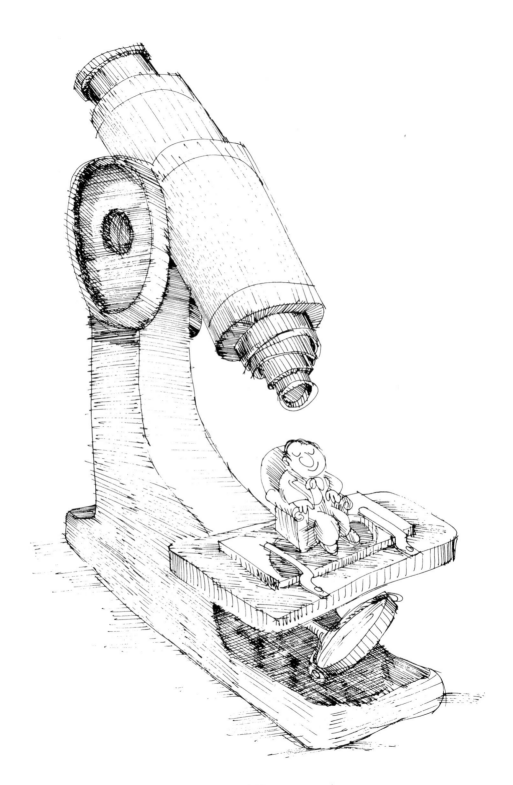

Any scientific proof?

One measure of how well we function is the level of anxiety—low anxiety means a feeling of inner security that enables us to interact with our environment in a harmonious way. During the TM technique, anxiety is greatly reduced.

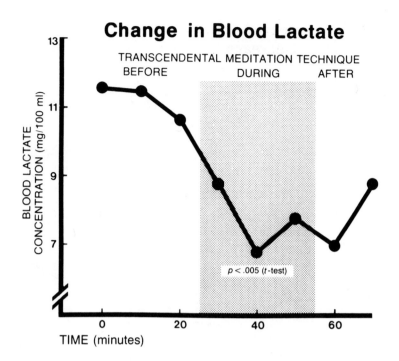

Change in Blood Lactate

TRANSCENDENTAL MEDITATION TECHNIQUE

BEFORE   DURING   AFTER

$p < .005$ (t-test)

BLOOD LACTATE CONCENTRATION (mg/100 ml)

TIME (minutes)

BIOCHEMISTRY OF DEEP REST

Finding: During the Transcendental Meditation technique the concentration of blood lactate markedly decreases and remains low some time after practice of the technique.

Interpretation: Decreased blood lactate is thought to indicate a profound state of muscular relaxation. A high concentration of lactate in the blood has been associated with anxiety neurosis, anxiety attacks, and high blood pressure. Therefore, the persistent decrease in lactate during and after the Transcendental Meditation technique is a biochemical correlate of an overall decrease in anxiety.

First Reference: Robert Keith Wallace and Herbert Benson, "The Physiology of Meditation," *Scientific American* 226, no. 2 (U.S.A.: 1972): 84–90.

Second Reference: Robert Keith Wallace, Herbert Benson, and Archie F. Wilson, "A Wakeful Hypometabolic Physiologic State," *American Journal of Physiology* 221, no. 3 (U.S.A.: 1971): 795–799.

As a result of the TM program, anxiety during activity is decreased.

135

Increased Inner Control,
Decreased Anxiety

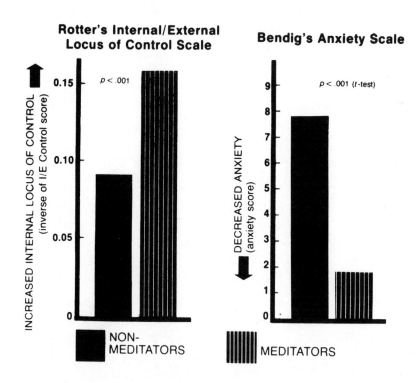

Rotter's Internal/External Locus of Control Scale

Bendig's Anxiety Scale

NON-MEDITATORS

MEDITATORS

INCREASED INNER CONTROL
DECREASED ANXIETY

Finding: Compared with a control group of non-meditators, subjects practicing the Transcendental Meditation technique demonstrated a more internal locus of control, as measured by Rotter's Internal/External (IE) Locus of Control Scale, and were less anxious, as measured by Bendig's Anxiety Scale.

Interpretation: Internal control as measured by Rotter's scale indicates the development of broader comprehension — insight into the causal connection between one's behavior and the environment and foresight into the consequences of one's behavior. High internal locus of control has been associated with psychological adaptability, low anxiety, and the ability to effectively extract and make use of information from a complex environment. Since the TM technique stabilizes the internal sense of self and improves the integration and thereby the effectiveness of thought and action, the meditator naturally feels a greater sense of control over his life.

Reference: Larry A. Hjelle, "Transcendental Meditation and Psychological Health," *Perceptual and Motor Skills* 39 (U.S.A: 1974): 623-628.

Decreased Anxiety

Institute for Personality and Ability Testing Anxiety Scale

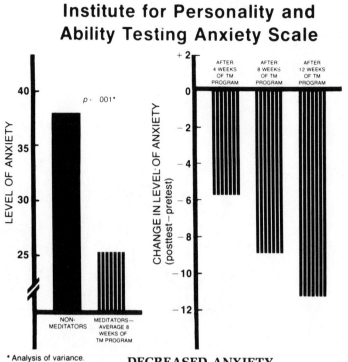

* Analysis of variance.

DECREASED ANXIETY

Finding: Research using the Institute for Personality and Ability Testing (IPAT) Anxiety Scale indicated that after beginning the Transcendental Meditation technique subjects showed a significant ($p. < .001$) decrease in anxiety level and exhibited significantly less anxiety than non-meditators. The reduction of anxiety was progressively greater with length of practice of the TM technique.

Interpretation: The Transcendental Meditation program produces a cumulative decrease in anxiety. Anxiety is associated with impairment of functioning in almost all areas of life — physiological, perceptual-motor, intellectual, and emotional. Anxiety also causes psychological rigidity and blockage of creativity. Therefore, a reduction in anxiety can be expected to be accompanied by greater availability of the individual's inherent resources in every area of life.

Reference: Zoe Lazar, Lawrence Farwell, and John T. Farrow, "The Effects of the Transcendental Meditation Program on Anxiety, Drug Abuse, Cigarette Smoking, and Alcohol Consumption," (Harvard University, Boston, Massachusetts, U.S.A.).

So our thoughts and feelings are more clearly and freely expressed.

Some other concrete improvements to health as a result of the TM program are:

139

Relief from Insomnia

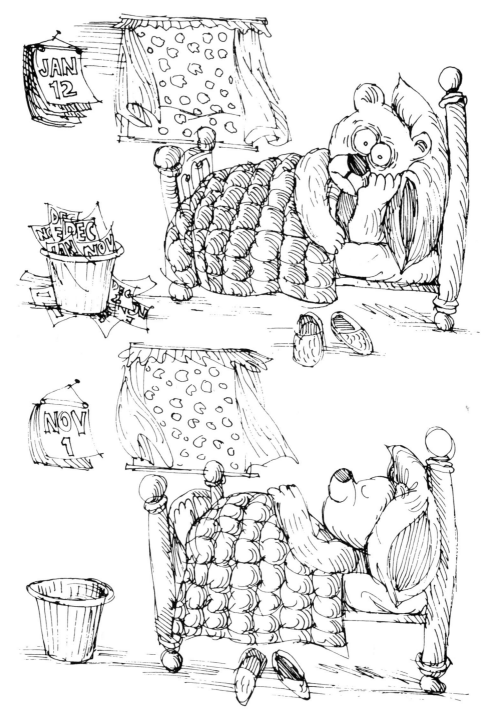

Change in Time of Sleep Onset

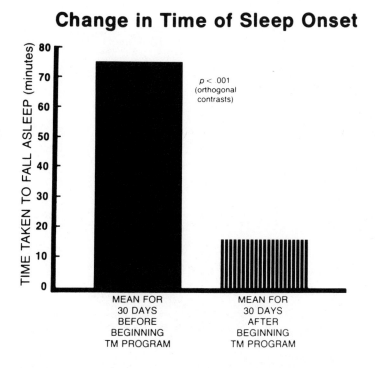

RELIEF FROM INSOMNIA

Finding: The Transcendental Meditation technique significantly reduced the time taken for insomniacs to fall asleep. As a therapy against insomnia, the Transcendental Meditation program was reported to be simple to administer, immediately effective, stable over time, and without unfavorable side effects.

Interpretation: The Transcendental Meditation technique relieves deep-seated stress from the nervous system on a direct physiological level. Consequently, it produces a wide range of beneficial effects without requiring specific attention to any one area. The effect seen here — greater regularity in the sleeping cycle — was subsequently shown to be stable throughout the first year of practice of the TM technique and can therefore not be accounted for by a placebo effect (see second reference). The results of this study reflect a stabilization of basic biological rhythms, one aspect of a holistic stabilization of daily life.

First Reference: Donald E. Miskiman, "The Treatment of Insomnia by the Transcendental Meditation Technique," (University of Alberta, Edmonton, Alberta, Canada).

Second Reference: Donald E. Miskiman, "Long-Term Effects of the Transcendental Meditation Technique on the Treatment of Insomnia," (University of Alberta, Edmonton, Alberta, Canada).

Even though the body may be very tired quite often tension interferes with sleep. The TM technique practiced for 15–20 minutes in the morning and again before supper removes tension so that the body can function in the most efficient and natural way. Because it removes tension, the TM technique helps us get a good night's sleep.

Beneficial Effects on Bronchial Asthma

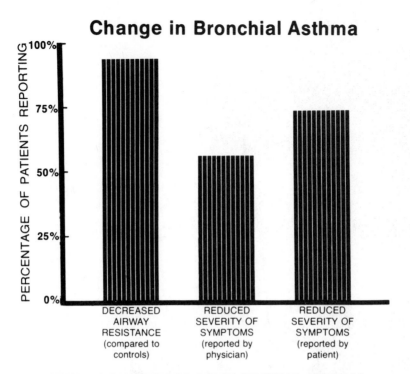

Change in Bronchial Asthma

PERCENTAGE OF PATIENTS REPORTING

- 100%
- 75%
- 50%
- 25%
- 0%

DECREASED AIRWAY RESISTANCE (compared to controls)

REDUCED SEVERITY OF SYMPTOMS (reported by physician)

REDUCED SEVERITY OF SYMPTOMS (reported by patient)

BENEFICIAL EFFECTS ON BRONCHIAL ASTHMA

Finding: After beginning the practice of the Transcendental Meditation technique 94 percent of a group of asthmatic patients showed improvement as determined by the physiological measurement of airway resistance. Fifty-five percent of the asthmatic patients showed improvement as reported by their personal physicians, and 74 percent showed improvement as reported by the patients themselves.

Interpretation: These results indicate that the Transcendental Meditation program is beneficial for patients with bronchial asthma. Bronchial asthma is one of a group of diseases the severity of which has been consistently correlated with the level of psychological stress of the individual. By systematically relieving stress, the Transcendental Meditation program promises to be an effective new adjunct to therapy for this and other psychosomatic diseases.

First Reference: Ron Honsberger and Archie F. Wilson, "The Effect of Transcendental Meditation upon Bronchial Asthma," *Clinical Research* 22, no. 2 (U.S.A.: 1973)

Second Reference: Ron Honsberger and Archie F. Wilson, "Transcendental Meditation in Treating Asthma," *Respiratory Therapy: The Journal of Inhalation Technology* 3, no. 6 (U.S.A.: 1973): 79–80.

Third Reference: Archie F. Wilson, Ron Honsberger, J.T. Chiu, and H.S. Novey, "Transcendental Meditation and Asthma," *Respiration* 32 (U.S.A.: 1973): 74–80.

Fourth Reference: Paul W. Corey, "Airway Conductance and Oxygen Consumption Changes Associated with Practice of the Transcendental Meditation Technique," (University of Colorado Medical Center, Denver, Colorado, U.S.A.).

What about new stresses?

A stronger nervous system doesn't acquire stress so easily.

Effective Interaction with the Environment

Habituation of Skin Resistance Responses

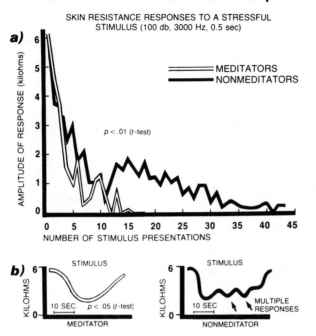

a) SKIN RESISTANCE RESPONSES TO A STRESSFUL STIMULUS (100 db, 3000 Hz, 0.5 sec)

AMPLITUDE OF RESPONSE (kilohms)

═══ MEDITATORS
━━━ NONMEDITATORS

$p < .01$ (*t*-test)

NUMBER OF STIMULUS PRESENTATIONS

b) KILOHMS
STIMULUS
10 SEC $p < .05$ (*t*-test)
MEDITATOR

KILOHMS
STIMULUS
10 SEC MULTIPLE RESPONSES
NONMEDITATOR

EFFECTIVE INTERACTION WITH THE ENVIRONMENT

Finding: In this study induced changes in skin resistance in response to a stressful stimulus were measured. Both the wave form of the individual response and the degree of habituation (reduced response) to repeated stimuli were recorded. Subjects practicing the Transcendental Meditation technique were found to habituate more rapidly to a series of auditory stresses (loud noises) than non-meditators (figure *a*). In addition, the wave form of the response to the first stress was significantly smoother and more stable in the meditators (figure *b*).

Interpretation: Those practicing the TM technique recover from stress more quickly than non-meditators. This faster habituation is known from other psychophysiological studies to be correlated with a more mature style of functioning of the nervous system and a more stable and expressive personality. In addition, meditators show a smoother style of response to stressful stimuli than non-meditators, indicating a more stable functioning of the nervous system in general. The practice of the Transcendental Meditation technique strengthens the individual's nervous system and allows him to function more effectively in a stressful environment.

Reference: David W. Orme-Johnson, "Autonomic Stability and Transcendental Meditation," *Psychosomatic Medicine* 35, no. 4 (U.S.A.: 1973): 341–349.

Faster Recovery from Sleep Deprivation

Response to Sleep Deprivation

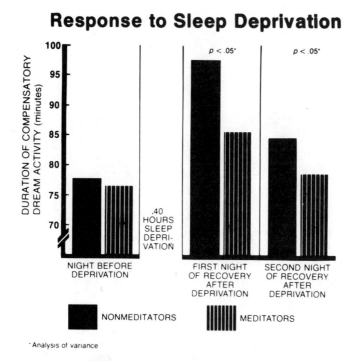

FASTER RECOVERY FROM SLEEP DEPRIVATION

Finding: Measurements showed that after 40 hours of sleep deprivation a group of subjects practicing the Transcendental Meditation technique recovered much more quickly than a control group of nonmeditators. Recovery was measured by duration of compensatory dreaming.

Interpretation: Sleep deprivation is a highly stressful experience, and compensatory dreaming is thought to be a form of stress release. The meditator's nervous system becomes more resilient and less subject to long-term disruption by a stressful experience. Faster recovery after exposure to stress of this type is valuable not only to people in everyday life but also to those in critical occupations, such as military, police, airline, and hospital personnel. This study also suggests that the TM technique may be helpful in the problem of jet lag.

Reference: Donald E. Miskiman, "The Effect of the Transcendental Meditation Technique on Compensatory Paradoxical Sleep," (University of Alberta, Edmonton, Alberta, Canada).

Something that is stressful when we're weak or tired can be dealt with easily when we're strong and alert. TM'ers recover more quickly from stressful situations.

149

Lower Hospital Admissions

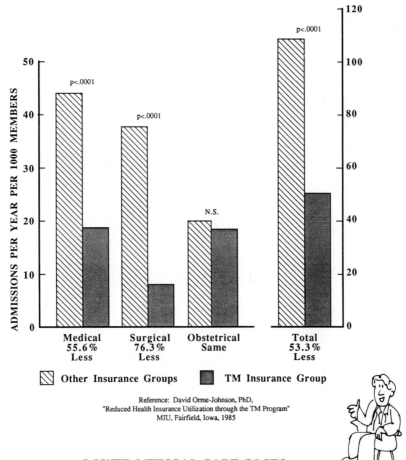

Reference: David Orme-Johnson, PhD,
"Reduced Health Insurance Utilization through the TM Program"
MIU, Fairfield, Iowa, 1985

LOWER MEDICAL CARE COSTS

This chart shows health care utilization statistics from a major health insurance carrier comparing the TM Insurance Group (regular practitioners of the Transcendental Meditation program) and Other Insurance Groups (the mean of all Iowa insurance groups with the same carrier). Hospital admissions for the TM Insurance Group were 55.6% less than the average for Other Insurance Groups for medical, 76.3% less for surgical, similar for obstetrical and 53.3% less for total admissions. The TM Insurance Group had lower admissions rates than even the lowest of the comparison groups on medical, surgical and total admissions. The TM Insurance Group, whose members are geographically distributed throughout the U.S.A., had a 68.8% lower hospital admissions rate than the mean for the U.S. as a whole and a 73.1% lower admissions rate than Iowa.

Reference: David W. Orme-Johnson, "Reduced Health Insurance Utilization through the Transcendental Meditation Program," (submitted for publication, 1986).

151

What's the bottom line here?

Simple. With TM, we stay healthier. And we continue to be healthy as we get older (see pages 268-273). This means that we see the doctor less often, go to the hospital less often, and have a shorter stay if we do go. At a time when health care costs are rising very quickly, TM is something we can do that will help us stay healthy, naturally.

Less Illness

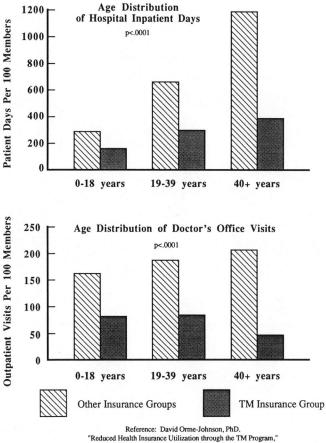

Age Distribution of Hospital Inpatient Days

p<.0001

Patient Days Per 100 Members

0-18 years   19-39 years   40+ years

Age Distribution of Doctor's Office Visits

p<.0001

Outpatient Visits Per 100 Members

0-18 years   19-39 years   40+ years

Other Insurance Groups   TM Insurance Group

Reference: David Orme-Johnson, PhD.
"Reduced Health Insurance Utilization through the TM Program,"
MIU, Fairfield, Iowa, 1985

INCREASED RESISTANCE TO DISEASE

The rates of hospital inpatient days and outpatient visits typically increase with age, as can be seen above in the statistics for Other Insurance Groups. The TM Insurance Group, however, not only showed much lower hospitalization rates than Other Insurance Groups in all age categories but also showed less of an increase of utilization with age, suggesting a slowing of the aging process through regular practice of the TM program.

Reference: David W. Orme-Johnson, "Reduced Health Insurance Utilization through the Transcendental Meditation Program," (submitted for publication, 1986).

This is because of the growth of stability and adaptability with TM.

But I'm enjoying life already! Why should I practice the TM program?

The TM program produces rapid growth, expansion, evolution, increased intelligence, energy, creativity, happiness. It is not necessary to have a *deficiency* in any of these values to enjoy having more. No matter how energetic, intelligent, and creative we are, we enjoy life when we become *more* energetic, intelligent, and creative.

This is Growth—a Fundamental of Progress.

GROWTH

PHYSIOLOGICAL GROWTH

Through the practice of the TRANSCENDENTAL MEDITATION technique, physiological growth—more efficient and effective physiological functioning—increases, as indicated by:

    growing strength and orderliness of brain functioning

    growing cardiovascular efficiency

    growing respiratory efficiency

    growing resistance to disease

    growing refinement of perception

    growing stability of the autonomic nervous system

    growing neuromuscular efficiency

    growing effectiveness in sports

    growing physiological adaptability, stability, integration, and purification

The metabolic rate decreases more during the TRANSCENDENTAL MEDITATION technique than during sleep, yet the brain wave patterns during meditation indicate a state of alertness rather than the dullness of sleep. The addition of this unique state of restful alertness to one's daily routine of rest and activity has been found to promote the growth of a superior quality of physiological functioning.

It is our daily experience that rest is the procedure for increasing physiological efficiency and effectiveness. Inefficient functioning of the physical system during the waking state, experienced as fatigue and dullness, is transformed through the mechanics of the sleep state into efficient physiological functioning, experienced as liveliness and clarity of the mind. This day-by-day rejuvenation of the system supports growing physiological efficiency.

The TRANSCENDENTAL MEDITATION technique works by the same natural principle, increasing physiological efficiency through rest. Because the TRANSCENDENTAL MEDITATION technique produces an even deeper rest than sleep, it is not surprising that the growth of physiological efficiency and effectiveness is greatly enhanced in meditators.

These physiological changes account for the psychological changes.

PSYCHOLOGICAL GROWTH

Through the practice of the TRANSCENDENTAL MEDITATION technique, psychological growth—the development of full potential of thinking, understanding, and feeling—is enhanced and enriched, as indicated by:

growing creativity

growing intelligence

growing efficiency and staying power

growing academic performance

growing learning ability

growing orderliness of thinking

growing spontaneity and capacity for intimate contact

growing self-actualization

growing self-esteem

growing inner control

growing sociability and friendliness

growing emotional stability and self-sufficiency

growing innovation

growing tolerance

growing individuality

This holistic value of psychological growth involving the simultaneous development of the abilities of thinking, understanding, and feeling is called evolution of consciousness. Growth is restricted when the process of growth starts to offer stress. Relative growth alone, untouched by the field of the Absolute, provides no opportunity for the full expression of creative intelligence. This makes it obvious that the growth of awareness of the absolute phase of life is vital, for the relative growth is so insane that it stops its own path. It is made sane by the growth of consciousness, and then it ceases to generate resistance on its own path; instead, it accelerates its speed and arrives at the goal quickly—the goal of fulfillment, the resultant value of the evolution of consciousness.

These physiological and psychological changes account for the sociological changes.

SOCIOLOGICAL GROWTH

Through the practice of the TRANSCENDENTAL MEDITATION technique, sociological growth—the growth of harmony in society—is accelerated and enriched, as indicated by:

    growing sociability

    improving interpersonal relationships

    growing productivity and improving performance in organizations

    growing job satisfaction

    growing social adequacy

    growing naturalness and outgoingness

    growing effectiveness of rehabilitation

    improved quality of life

The potential for the growth of individual consciousness is enormous and, on the basis of developed individual awareness through the TRANSCENDENTAL MEDITATION program, the growth of achievement and fulfillment possible in society is virtually unlimited. The achievements of society leading up to modern times are impressive even though psychologists have agreed that only a fraction of human potential is being utilized. When full human potential is developed through the implementation of Maharishi's World Plan, the world will enjoy an age of unprecedented brilliance—generation after generation.

These physiological, psychological, and sociological changes account for the ecological changes.

158

ECOLOGICAL GROWTH

Ecological growth is the expression of growing wholeness of life. For man this ecological wholeness has its value in:

the development of wholeness of life within himself:

self-actualization

the development of the ability to appreciate wholeness in his environment:

broadened awareness, increased perceptual ability, and increased learning ability

the development of the ability to refrain from disrupting regulatory mechanisms responsible for the preservation of ecological stability and growth:

increased intelligence, respect, and self-sufficiency

the development of the ability to project and promote life-supporting influences to enrich and strengthen those fundamental mechanisms in nature responsible for all ecological stability and growth:

increased liveliness, naturalness, spontaneity, innovation, energy, creativity, good humor, and cordiality

This is how man, the most influential member of the ecosphere, contributes maximum effect to ecological growth through his daily practice of the TRANSCENDENTAL MEDITATION technique. Ecological growth—the expression of wholeness of life in man and in nature—constitutes the supreme state of all growth. This supreme state of growth has traditionally been known as spiritual value.

The TM technique improves perception, for example. We all enjoy perceiving more clearly. I'm sure you've noticed that some days, when you're rested and fresh, the world seems alive! A beautiful place! Music seems more enchanting, a friend more delightful. This is just improved perception. Everyone wants that.

Couldn't that improved perception be overwhelming?

The TM program develops *all* aspects of human ability, spontaneously, in a balanced, integrated way. So we'll never find one quality developing at the expense of any other. To balance perception the TM program develops attention—the increased ability to focus.

Change in Field Independence

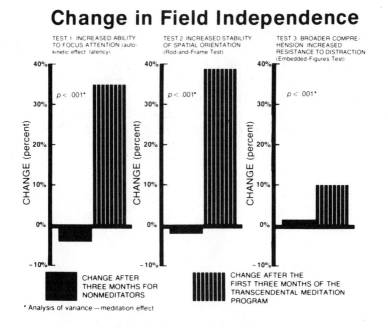

TEST 1: INCREASED ABILITY TO FOCUS ATTENTION (autokinetic effect latency)

TEST 2: INCREASED STABILITY OF SPATIAL ORIENTATION (Rod-and-Frame Test)

TEST 3: BROADER COMPREHENSION, INCREASED RESISTANCE TO DISTRACTION (Embedded-Figures Test)

CHANGE AFTER THREE MONTHS FOR NONMEDITATORS

CHANGE AFTER THE FIRST THREE MONTHS OF THE TRANSCENDENTAL MEDITATION PROGRAM

* Analysis of variance — meditation effect

BROADER COMPREHENSION AND IMPROVED ABILITY TO FOCUS ATTENTION

Finding: In this study three tests were administered that directly measure field independence, the ability to focus attention on specific objects without being distracted by the environment of the objects. Meditators changed significantly in the direction of increased field independence after practicing the Transcendental Meditation technique for three months, compared with a non-meditating control group.

The latency of the autokinetic effect measures the time it takes a subject to perceive movement of a spot of light; the Rod-and-Frame Test measures the ability to orient a rod to true vertical position against a tilted frame; and the Embedded-Figures Test measures the ability to perceive simple figures embedded in a complex background.

Interpretation: These measures indicate the development of field independence, the ability to analytically perceive an item embedded in a complex context. Researchers have found that persons with greater field independence have the following characteristics: greater ability to assimilate and structure experience; greater organization of mind and cognitive clarity; improved memory; greater creative expression; stable internal frame of reference; stable standards, attitudes, judgement, and sentiments without continuous reference to external standards; differentiation of inner and outer; autonomic stability; more assertiveness. All these characteristics are indications of improved neurological organization and, consequently, more evolved consciousness. This improvement in meditators is all the more remarkable because it was previously believed that these basic perceptual abilities do not improve beyond early adulthood.

First Reference: Kenneth R. Pelletier, "The Effects of the Transcendental Meditation Program on Perceptual Style: Increased Field Independence," (University of California School of Medicine, San Francisco, California, U.S.A.).

Second Reference: Kenneth R. Pelletier, "Influence of Transcendental Meditation upon Autokinetic Perception," *Perceptual and Motor Skills 39* (U.S.A.: 1974): 1031–1034.

One feature of this chart is particularly interesting—the Rod and Frame test in the middle section of the chart. In this experiment the subject sits in a dark room. In front of him is a lighted square that is tilted so it does not represent horizontal and vertical. Inside the square is a rod which the subject must adjust to true vertical. This means that he has to ignore his impression of the tilted environment, the lighted frame, and depend on his own inner perceptions—his sense of gravity and true vertical. The graph illustrates that the subjects scored much higher after taking the TM program.

So what does this really show?

It shows that even though perception does become increasingly refined, inner stability and discrimination are also improved. Psychologists call this "field independence"; that is, the subject acts from his own information and inner awareness, and thus he can successfully disregard irrelevant or distracting information from his environment, or "field."

Other research has established that people who are field-independent are active, independent, not submissive, and less anxious. They have fewer spontaneous galvanic skin responses (see page 103), more self-esteem, and more favorable beliefs about human nature.

Psychologists call such people "self-actualized." This means that their own inner nature, or inner potential, is actualized, made real. TM'ers grown in self-actualization.

Increased Self-Actualization

Northridge Developmental Scale

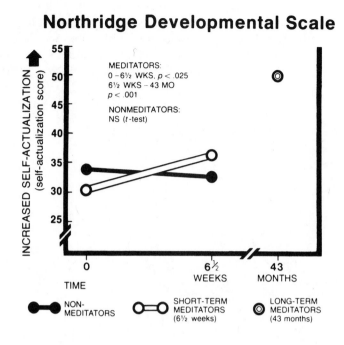

INCREASED SELF-ACTUALIZATION

Finding: Subjects practicing the Transcendental Meditation technique for an average of 1.5 months showed a significant increase in self-actualization compared with a group of non-meditators, as measured by the Northridge Developmental Scale. The level of self-actualization was highest in long-term (average 43 months) meditators (as denoted by the double circle on the chart), indicating that the benefits of the Transcendental Meditation program are cumulative.

Interpretation: Growth of self-actualization as defined by this test includes the development of the following qualities: open, receptive, caring attitude; cheerfulness and good humor; predominance of positive thinking; spontaneity and freshness of appreciation; self-sufficiency; loss of fear of death; affective readiness for developing consciousness; discovery of opportunities for creativity; acceptance of self, nature, and others; conscious sense of destiny. This study shows that the Transcendental Meditation programme allows the personality to unfold naturally in the direction of self-actualization on the basis of an increasingly refined nervous system.

Reference: Phillip C. Ferguson and John C. Gowan. "Psychological Findings on Transcendental Meditation," (Paper presented to the California State Psychological Association, Fresno, California. U.S.A., 1974), *Journal of Humanistic Psychology* (in press).

Self-actualized people are inner-directed; they're motivated from within. They enjoy solitude, and they enjoy interaction with other people. They have superior perception of reality and enjoy a fresh, spontaneous appreciation of life. They're in command of their resources, spontaneous and fulfilled.

Whew! All those benefits!

Fortunately the TM program integrates all these changes into one's life in a natural and balanced way. This brings us to our last Fundamental of Progress, Integration.

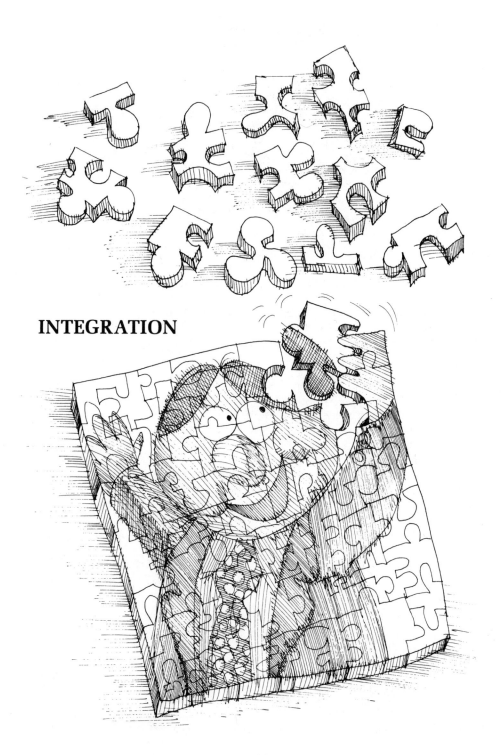

INTEGRATION

PHYSIOLOGICAL INTEGRATION

Through the practice of the TRANSCENDENTAL MEDITATION technique, physiological integration—integration of the physical system and its smooth coordinated functioning—increases, as indicated by:

neuromuscular integration

integrated functioning of the sensory apparatus, indicated by improved perception and attention

integrated state of "restful alertness" as indicated by simultaneous changes in:

metabolic rate

biochemistry

electrophysiology

electroencephalography

integrated functioning of the left and right hemispheres of the brain, implying functional integration of the analytic and verbal skills of the left hemisphere with the synthetic and spatial skills of the right hemisphere

integrated functioning of the front and back of the brain, implying improved, integrated functioning of thinking and thought-action coordination

increased stability, harmony, balance, and coherence of brain functioning

increased integration of the immune system resulting in improved resistance to disease

integration of mind and body as indicated by:

faster reactions

superior perceptual-motor performance

improved athletic performance

The observations mentioned above, with reference to coordinated brain functioning, suggest increasing integration of both aspects of the brain waves—their structure and function—total integration resulting from the TRANSCENDENTAL MEDITATION technique.

These physiological changes account for the psychological changes.

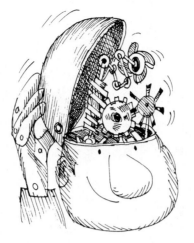

PSYCHOLOGICAL INTEGRATION

Through the practice of the TRANSCENDENTAL MEDITATION technique, psychological integration—the integration of all faculties of the mind: thinking, understanding, and feeling—increases, as indicated by:

increased integration of intellect:
increased intelligence
increased learning ability
improved academic performance
increased orderliness of thinking
improved discriminative capacity

increased integration of heart and mind

increased integration of action:
increased creativity
increased innovation
increased energy level
increased efficiency

increased integration of personality:
increased self-actualization
increased naturalness and spontaneity
increased wholeness and unity of person
increased individuality

increased productivity
increased perceptual-motor performance
faster reactions
improved athletic performance

All faculties of the mind—thinking, feeling, and understanding—have a common basis in pure consciousness. For profound integration, it is necessary to take the mind towards this unifying field of consciousness.

Applying this phenomenon of integration of the mind to the practicalities of business, industry, and progress, what we find is that although productivity and progress necessitate both routine work and a broad basis of comprehension, the paradox of productivity is that the act of habitually focusing the mind during routine work keeps awareness within narrow boundaries, restricting broad comprehension. This restriction to the full expression of creative intelligence makes life uncomfortable and remains as a seed for frustration and discontent, which expresses itself in various modes of suffering and negativity in life. The experience of unbounded awareness during the TRANSCENDENTAL MEDITATION technique counterbalances the narrowing influence of routine work on the mind. In this way, one can maintain the benefit of routine work and eliminate the restricting influence on broad comprehension.

These physiological and psychological changes account for the sociological changes.

169

SOCIOLOGICAL INTEGRATION

Through the practice of the TRANSCENDENTAL MEDITATION technique, sociological integration—the harmonious coexistence, coordinated growth, and mutual fulfillment of the different behavioral patterns of society—increases, as indicated by:

more rewarding and productive interpersonal relationships among executives and employees

increased integrating influences:

more respect

increased cordiality

increased tolerance

increased contentment

increased sociability

increased naturalness and spontaneity

decreased discordant influences:

decreased irritability

decreased anxiety

decreased social inadequacy

decreased stress and increased acceptable social behavior of prisoners

reduced use of alcohol, cigarettes, and nonprescribed drugs

decreased crime rate

Social disharmony and discord in the family of nations, on the basis of national boundaries made rigid on the level of awareness of the people, produce the same influence as grows through routine work. (Refer to Psychological Integration.) All international conflicts and wars throughout the ages and the continuing situation of wars and conflicts in every generation are, from this point of view, based on the nonavailability of unbounded awareness, which can counterbalance the rigidity caused by the importance laid on national boundaries to the exclusion of international significance. Now with the TRANSCENDENTAL MEDITATION technique, unbounded awareness is available to all; the national boundaries will enjoy the flavor of international significance, and their narrowing influence will be neutralized. Here is the expression of the supreme value of sociological integration, which the TRANSCENDENTAL MEDITATION program is capable of providing.

These physiological, psychological, and sociological changes account for the ecological changes.

ECOLOGICAL INTEGRATION

Through the practice of the TRANSCENDENTAL MEDITATION technique, ecological integration—the wholeness of the individual's relationship with his environment—blossoms, as a result of the total effect of the practice, which increases:

    physiological integration

    psychological integration

    sociological integration

Air flowing over cool water takes the cold from the surface of the water and makes everything cool wherever it flows. The air flowing over hot water spreads the influence of heat all around. This explains the way in which the quality of the individual spreads in his environment. The TRANSCENDENTAL MEDITATION program, developing unbounded awareness, produces such a holistic value of integration in the individual that all fields of life—physiological, psychological, and sociological—are integrated simultaneously, and this produces a lively, concentrated, and powerful center of integration in the individual from where the influence of integration spontaneously radiates all around the whole of the environment and reverberates through the whole of the ecosphere. The process of ecological integration continues as the practice of the TRANSCENDENTAL MEDITATION technique continues—twice a day meditation, twice a day integration.

171

All this sounds very scientific, but I always thought meditation had something to do with "enlightenment."

There's nothing unscientific or mystical about enlightenment. Enlightenment simply means a state of mind and nervous system in which 100% of our potential is available for use. Another way to look at it is that enlightenment is the state of awareness produced by a nervous system with no stress and strain, a mind using full mental potential. Scientific research has shown that enlightenment is a very specific, permanent state of enjoyment. Consciousness is not restricted by structural or chemical imbalances in the system and can shine forth in its true value. This is all so different from our usual 5–15% efficiency that this beautiful state of life has become legend. Now, thanks to the TM program, it is available for everyone to enjoy.

**But I thought to gain enlightenment you had to give away all your posses-
sions, perform rigid disciplines and live in a cave for the rest of your life.**

The severity of that life style doesn't sound very enticing, does it? This
misunderstanding of the road to enlightenment is why for thousands of years
people with responsibilities in society have thought enlightenment to be
difficult and impractical—something for monks and recluses, requiring fan-
tastic will power.

We in this generation are deeply indebted to Maharishi and to his teacher,
Guru Dev, for providing an effortless, extremely rapid technique for everyone
to achieve this most practical and basic of human goals.

This one of Maharishi's main points, that enlightenment—using one's full
potential—is *everyone's* birthright and that it can be easily attained by us all.

How does the TM program make one more creative?

The TM technique increases our contact with the source of creativity within us. Also, it removes stress from the nervous system, making us more sensitive and more responsive to our environment. Greater intelligence, perception, and clarity of mind automatically bring expanded creativity.

A common misconception about creativity is that it is limited to the rather narrow field of "the arts." Creativity is a daily experience—an exciting way of dealing with all the situations of living. To create is to feel alive.

Another misconception is that creativity depends on suffering or tension. Actually, tension inhibits creativity, just as it interferes with every other area of life. The more sensitive, responsive, stable, and intelligent we are, the more creative we will be. The more we perceive and understand, the more we can express and share.

Torrance Test of Creative Thinking
Three Aspects of Creativity

INCREASED CREATIVITY

Finding: The Torrance Test of Creative Thinking (TTCT), Verbal Form A, was used to compare 44 subjects practicing the Transcendental Meditation technique for an average of 18 months with 41 subjects who had just learned the Transcendental Meditation technique. The two groups were equivalent in age, sex, education, and income level. The long-term meditators scored significantly higher (p<.01) on all three scales of the TTCT—Fluency, Flexibility, and Originality—indicating that practice of the Transcendental Meditation technique increases creativity.

Interpretation: The TTCT was developed to measure the type of creative thinking process described by eminent scientific researchers, inventors, and creative writers. Psychologists such as Carl Rogers and Abraham Maslow have associated this type of creativity with increased self-actualization, which has also been found by independent studies to result from the Transcendental Meditation program. These findings give objective validation to the statement that the Transcendental Meditation program systematically develops creative intelligence by providing a means to directly experience the source of creativity in the mind. The aspects of creativity measured here—fluency, flexibility, and originality—may be associated with integration, adaptability, and growth, three of the fundamentals of progress that are enhanced by the Transcendental Meditation technique.

Reference: Michael J. MacCallum, "The Transcendental Meditation Program and Creativity" (California State University, Long Beach, California, U.S.A.).

177

Does this creativity extend to my personal relationships?

Absolutely. It begins with perception. When our nervous system is free from stress and our mind is clear and expanded, we perceive the world as a joyful place. We appreciate life more.

This appreciation grows until it can only be referred to as love. Love is the automatic, ultimate appreciation of a person, place, or thing.

We send out love; we get love in return. "For every action there is an equal and opposite reaction." We love, we receive love. We hate, and find hate returned. This is simple physics. Nothing in the universe exists in isolation. All our thoughts and actions affect every atom in creation, and every atom responds in kind.

So we should try to love.

No. There should be no trying involved. Loving is the natural state of man. Man was not born for suffering. Man was born to enjoy life, to radiate this enjoyment for all to share. This is the natural, spontaneous experience of evolution: greater joy and happiness, and increased expression of this fulfillment.

It is this natural tendency to radiate goodness when we are feeling happy that is the basis of the social benefits of the Transcendental Meditation program. Like a current running through a filament, when joy enlivens the human nervous system, the system has no choice but to express this joy, this understanding, this appreciation of life.

And this joy comes from——

The expanded potential of the mind and the increased clarity of the nervous system. Radiation of warmth, love, happiness is the natural result of joy. There is no "mood making" here.

"Mood making"?

When you try to love, what you're doing is "trying," not loving. You create a "mood" of loving. In return, you receive a "mood," not love. Have you ever visited an office in which no one really likes anyone else, and everyone knows no one likes anyone, yet everyone smiles and pretends to be loving just the same?

No one is fooled by artificial warmth, not really.

Another danger of "mood making" is a loss of reality—life becomes a game that seems to have no end. Now we have a simple technique that makes individuals individual, makes the enjoyment of life genuine, makes relationships real.

With the TM technique the nervous system is spontaneously relieved of stress, the mind automatically expanded. This leads to natural appreciation, which grows to effortless loving. You will notice there is no trying involved in this entire process. From the technique through the inevitable sharing of love, every step is effortless, natural, spontaneous.

The growth of awareness and sensitivity, using the TM technique, is systematic. Our emotions do not become "mechanized," but the process that spontaneously leads to more and more loving is scientific and predictable.

Are we still capable of maintaining one-to-one intimate relationships?

Still capable? *Finally* capable!

All relationships are enhanced and warmed if one or more of the individuals is practicing the TM program. It's only logical: people who are sensitive, aware, lively, and warm are a joy to be around. On days when you're feeling good, it's easy to be with your friends. It's easy to love. It flows naturally. As we follow the TM program, we feel good more and more often. We draw the best people to us, and draw the best from those people.

All the limitations we once felt in our intimate relationships—anger, jealousy, insecurity, fear, depression—significantly decrease. We become understanding, patient, tender—truly loving. And we don't have to try for it—it's automatic.

Development of Personality

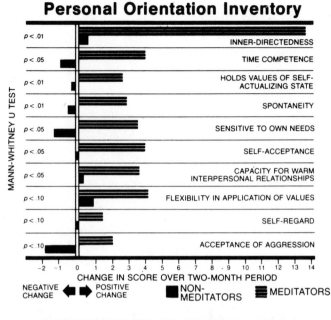

Personal Orientation Inventory

MANN-WHITNEY U TEST		
p < .01		INNER-DIRECTEDNESS
p < .05		TIME COMPETENCE
p < .01		HOLDS VALUES OF SELF-ACTUALIZING STATE
p < .01		SPONTANEITY
p < .05		SENSITIVE TO OWN NEEDS
p < .05		SELF-ACCEPTANCE
p < .05		CAPACITY FOR WARM INTERPERSONAL RELATIONSHIPS
p < .10		FLEXIBILITY IN APPLICATION OF VALUES
p < .10		SELF-REGARD
p < .10		ACCEPTANCE OF AGGRESSION

CHANGE IN SCORE OVER TWO-MONTH PERIOD

NEGATIVE CHANGE ← → POSITIVE CHANGE ■ NON-MEDITATORS ≡ MEDITATORS

DEVELOPMENT OF PERSONALITY

Finding: Subjects practicing the Transcendental Meditation technique, measured once prior to beginning the technique and again two months later, showed significant positive improvement in the following traits when compared with a matched control group of non-meditators: inner-directedness, time competence, self-actualization, spontaneity, sensitivity to one's needs, self-acceptance, and capacity for warm interpersonal relationships. The test used was the Personal Orientation Inventory (POI). Two independent studies also using the POI confirmed these results.

Interpretation: The POI was developed by Shostrom to measure Maslow's concept of self-actualization. Maslow defines self-actualization as a high level of maturity, health, and fulfillment; transcendence of deficiencies; a clearer, more efficient perception of reality; more openness to experience; increased integration, wholeness, and unity of person; increased spontaneity, expressiveness, aliveness; a real self; increased objectivity, detachment, transcendence of self; ability to fuse concreteness and abstractness; ability to love; a firm identity, increased autonomy, and resistance to enculturation. All the personality changes brought about by the Transcendental Meditation program are clearly in the direction of what is generally recognized as the develpment of a healthy, self-actualized personality.

First Reference: Sanford Nidich, William Seeman, and Thomas Dreskin, "Influence of Transcendental Meditation: A Replication," *Journal of Counseling Psychology* 20, no. 6 (U.S.A.: 1973): 565-566.

Second Reference: William Seeman, Sanford Nidich, and Thomas Banta, "Influence of Transcendental Meditation on a Measure of Self-Actualization," *Journal of Counseling Psychology* 19, no. 3 (U.S.A.: 1972): 184-187.

Third Reference: Larry A. Hjelle, "Transcendental Meditation and Psychological Health," *Perceptual and Motor Skills* 39 (U.S.A: 1974): 623-628.

Chapter 4

Learning the TM technique

If I decide to do it, how do I go about learning the TM technique?

You can learn the Transcendental Meditation technique in seven steps. They are:

A. Introductory steps:
1. *Introductory lecture.* If you've read our book thus far you are already acquainted with the introductory material (What can the TM program do for me?).
2. *Preparatory lecture.* This lecture is about the mechanics of the TM technique itself — specific explanations of how the technique works, how it differs from other techniques, where it comes from, how it is taught, and why it is taught in that way.
3. *Personal interview.* After the preparatory lecture, you meet with a teacher of the TM program, clear up any questions you may have and schedule a convenient time for personal instruction.

B. Four consecutive days of instruction (two hours each day):
4. *Personal instruction.* This is the private session where you learn the TM technique from your teacher, who has been trained and qualified by Maharishi.
5. *First day checking.* In this seminar session you receive further instruction and answers to your questions about your experiences while discussing practical details about the TM program.
6. *Second day checking.* The seminar discusses the mechanics of the process of the TM technique and the release of stress in the light of their experience with the practice.
7. *Third day checking.* This seminar session explores the goal of the TM program — life free from stress, with the full use of mental and physical potential.

185

Is that all?

About ten days after you begin, you'll come back for another meeting with your class and teacher to get the answers to any questions that may have occurred to you, and to be sure that the practice is going well. And you can come in any time, to any Capital of the Age of Enlightenment (see pages 311, 312), as often as you like. There, regular checking is available to make sure that the practice of the TM technique is correct. Also, centers have many optional lectures on the TM technnique, the whole TM program, and the Science of Creative Intelligence.

Are there any requirements for starting the Transcendental Meditation program?

Yes.

I knew there was a catch!

Three catches. The first and most important is a commitment of time. You must be able to go to all the sessions — both of the first two lectures, the interview, and most important, all four consecutive sessions of instruction. And you should set aside 15-20 minutes, twice a day, for the regular practice of the TM technique.

What if I haven't learned how in four sessions?

You learn how in the *first* session! The next three are for confirming your understanding, and explaining how the technique works. It is very easy to learn, and the teaching procedures are specifically designed to ensure that everyone learns quickly and easily. If you'd like more instruction or have any questions about the TM technique, you can come into the center for verification of the practice — we call it "checking." The entire TM program, including unlimited checking and many lecture programs, is included in the course fee.

Course fee?

As of 1986, the course fee in the USA is $390 per person. Couples and their dependent children may all start together for $590. The fee for those retired on a fixed income is $190 and for full-time college students is $145. Children age 10 through high school may learn the technique for $75. Children between four and ten are asked to bring two weeks' allowance.

What's the money used for?

All the organizations that teach the TM program are nonprofit, tax-exempt, educational organizations. There are costs involved in teaching the technique and in maintaining an organization so that anyone can learn — renting halls and rooms, printing pamphlets and posters, advertising, teachers' salaries — all basic expenses which each person helps to meet when he begins the TM course.

As we mentioned, the one-time course fee includes the four sessions of instruction, and unlimited checking of the TM technique, plus the optional weekly meetings and other activities at each center.

For happiness, growing every day, it's quite reasonable, especially when compared to other ways we spend money for personal development and enjoyment in life.

So that's two requirements — what's number three?

The third is that you refrain from any nonprescription "recreational" drugs for fifteen days prior to personal instruction. By nonprescription "recreational" drugs we mean marijuana, LSD, amphetamines, barbiturates, narcotics — anything your doctor did not prescribe.

Why no nonprescription drugs for fifteen days?

Drugs alter perception and can damage the nervous system. It's necessary for perception to be as natural as possible so that the TM technique can be learned most easily and effectively.

But the effects of these drugs seem to wear off in a few hours, or at most, a few days. Why wait fifteen days?

The very subtle effects of these drugs do persist long after the more obvious effects. Scientific research on these drugs shows that it takes at least fifteen days for the system to be reasonably clear of residual effects. Experience teaching the TM technique to hundreds of thousands of people has shown this clarity to be essential for the right start of the technique.

What about aspirin, or prescription drugs?

It's not necessary to stop taking aspirin and other "over the counter' medicines. Also, we don't interfere with the doctors' prescriptions—if a doctor prescribes some drug, it's important for maintaining health.

May I drink before I begin the TM technique?

Not within a few hours of beginning—and we suggest that you not drink more than your usual amount of alcohol for a day or two before you begin.

What about cigarettes?

Tobacco doesn't seem to interfere with the effective start of the TM technique.

Do I need to meet all these requirements just to come to the introductory lecture?

No—the introductory and preparatory lectures are to introduce the TM program, clear away misconceptions, and to give some basic information about the practice. You can come to these any time, even several times if you like. Of course, there is no charge for these talks. When you decide you'd like to start the technique, then the requirements become relevant.

How does the TM technique work?

The important thing about the TM technique is that it produces an experience—a concrete, specific, lively experience. The description of an experience is bound to be abstract. As we mentioned before, imagine describing the taste of a strawberry. But the experience of a strawberry is very real—as is the experience of the TM technique.

Already, we've said many times that the TM technique is effortless, spontaneous and natural. Now to be more specific, the TM technique works on the basis of the natural tendency of the mind.

Natural tendency of the mind?

Yes, to enjoy more and more. As we have explained, the field of pure creative intelligence is the source of all energy and intelligence, so it is very charming and the attention naturally goes there. All we need is a technique.

Thoughts come from this source, the field of pure creative intelligence. All thoughts, as we usually experience them, are directed outward, through thinking and speech, and then into action. During the TM technique, we use a vehicle, a specific thought, called a "mantra." Because of the nature of the vehicle, and the way we are taught to experience it, the mind automatically goes within, following the thought of the mantra back to the source of all thought. Each "step" toward pure consciousness is more and more fulfilling, and the final step — the experience of pure creative intelligence — is the most fulfilling of all.

Mantra?

"Mantra" means a specific sound, with no meaning, the effects of which are known for the individual in every way — mentally, physically, and environmentally. These mantras come from an ancient tradition which assures their beneficial effectiveness. They are taught in a very specific way. Everyone learns individually and privately, from a teacher who has been trained and qualified by Maharishi. The teaching procedure is a very simple exchange of information and instructions between the teacher and the student. The teacher gives some instruction and the student follows it. Then, the teacher asks some question and, on the basis of the answer, gives some further instruction. The student is lead *innocently* — that's the key word — to the experience of transcending, the experience of pure creative intelligence.

What does the TM experience feel like?

Different people describe the experience in different ways—very quiet, deeply peaceful, calm, so easy to do, etc. But is important to remember that we practice the technique for its results in activity, not for any particular experience *during* the practice.

If it is so easy, why don't you just print a list of mantras and a few directions and I can learn from a book?

There are several reasons. First, there's that interchange between teacher and student which ensures that you have correct experiences. Second, it's necessary that the mantra be personally selected by a trained teacher, and that it be imparted properly and usefully.

So you need the correct mantra, properly selected, properly given, and properly used. These three elements are essentials for effortless, effective practice of the Transcendental Meditation technique.

Where do the mantras come from?

They come from a very old tradition of great teachers that goes back thousands of years. The nearest teacher to us in this tradition is Maharishi's teacher, Guru Dev, His Divinity Swami Brahmananda Saraswati, who had the wisdom and insight to revive this great teaching.

Where does Maharishi come in?

Maharishi has been teaching continuously throughout the world since 1959. This has been in response to the tremendous need of our age for a simple technique to accomplish so much. Everywhere he goes, he inspires people with his vision of a world free from suffering. He personally trains and qualifies all teachers of the TM program and, through his inspiration he guides all phases of the movement.

What is the movement?

In each country, the TM program is coordinated by a Maharishi National Capital of the Age of Enlightenment. The TM technique is taught in each local Maharishi City Capital of the Age of Enlightenment through ten councils, which present the knowledge of the TM program to all areas of society:

Council for the Development of Consciousness — for presentations to the general public and to members of the clergy.

Council of National Law and Order — for presentations in the fields of law, justice and rehabilitation.

Council of Cultural Integrity, Invincibility and World Harmony — for presentations to the military, to cultural organizations, and to those concerned with international affairs.

Council of Education and Enlightenment — for presentations in the field of education: to students, faculty and administrators.

Council of Celebrations and Fulfillment — for presentations to those involved in all fields of creative expression, and for coordination of seasonal celebrations honoring outstanding individuals from every area of society.

Council of Prosperity and Progress — for presentations to business, management and industry.

Council of Information and Inspiration — for presentations to those in all fields of communication, including the media and public relations.

Council of All Possibilities: Research and Development — for presentations to those involved in science and technology.

Council for Capitals of the Age of Enlightenment — for presentations to all levels of government.

Council of Perfect Health and Longevity — for presentations in the field of health and medicine, and to athletic organizations.

Where do I go to learn the TM technique?

Write or call the nearest center on the list at the back of this book. They'll tell you the address of your local Capital of the Age of Enlightenment.

the TM Program:
Solution to All Problems?

All problems! You folks are mighty ambitious!

Consider how mankind has gone about solving problems so far. We examine the problem, think about it, do something. Perhaps what we do is effective, perhaps not. Perhaps in a little while it is obvious that the side effects of our "solution" are worse than the problem. Clearly, our world situation indicates that more creativity and intelligence are essential.

Consider the problem of darkness. Suppose a room is full of darkness, and those in the room want to eliminate the darkness. They might form a committee—THE COMMITTEE ON DARKNESS.

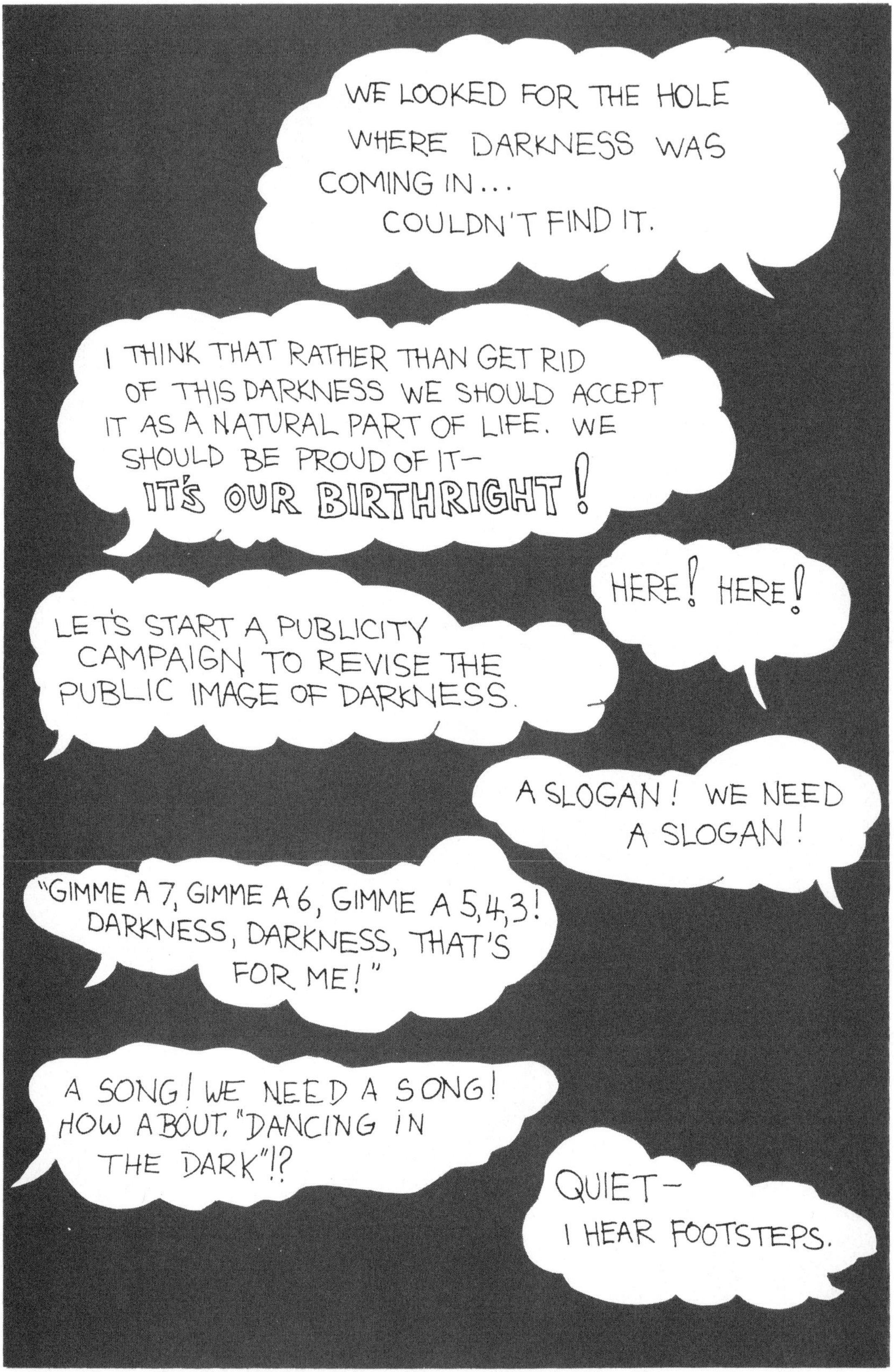
WE LOOKED FOR THE HOLE WHERE DARKNESS WAS COMING IN... COULDN'T FIND IT.
I THINK THAT RATHER THAN GET RID OF THIS DARKNESS WE SHOULD ACCEPT IT AS A NATURAL PART OF LIFE. WE SHOULD BE PROUD OF IT— IT'S OUR BIRTHRIGHT!
HERE! HERE!
LET'S START A PUBLICITY CAMPAIGN TO REVISE THE PUBLIC IMAGE OF DARKNESS.
A SLOGAN! WE NEED A SLOGAN!
"GIMME A 7, GIMME A 6, GIMME A 5,4,3! DARKNESS, DARKNESS, THAT'S FOR ME!"
A SONG! WE NEED A SONG! HOW ABOUT, "DANCING IN THE DARK"!?
QUIET— I HEAR FOOTSTEPS.

What the committee tried to do was solve the problem of darkness on the level of the problem.

This "problem" of darkness is simply the absence of light. We turn on the light and the problem of darkness is gone. This is the principle of introducing the "second element," which in this case is light.

Fine, but what does this have to do with the TM program?

The TM technique infuses strength, stability, creativity, and intelligence into human life. A problem is simply the inability to deal with some situation—when ability is increased, the "problem" becomes an easy task, a challenge, or even a pleasure. The TM program eliminates the root of all problems—weakness.

Interesting principle, but it still seems very impractical.

Alright, let's explore it a little further. We'll consider some of our current problems and explain how the TM program solves them.

What about the problem of education? Many students find it boring and a waste of time.

There are two important aspects of education: factual knowledge and individual ability. Most education today offers only one of these aspects the study of *facts* about this and that. But the more we study any field, the more we realize how much we do not know and the more we question the practical value of what we're learning. What's missing is the personal aspect, the development of the student's own *ability* to learn. The TM program provides this second aspect to education. It develops the capacity to know, expanding the "container" of knowledge.

When a student is practicing the TM program, every day his mind is fresher and more alert. Perception is keener and the intellect is sharper. The ability to integrate grows so that all knowledge can be constructively and holistically applied in such away that the student finds education enjoyable, relevant, and rewarding.

What about a job that involves a tremendous amount of routine. There doesn't seem to be much chance to display creative intelligence there.

Routine work is necessary for progress, yet we've all experienced the boredom and frustration that it brings. Whenever growth is obstructed, whenever creative intelligence does not find an opportunity for full expression in life, then we begin to feel uncomfortable. This discomfort is the seat of frustration, and this frustration is the basis of all problems in life.

What is needed is some way for awareness to grow, for creativity and intelligence to express themselves. The TM program does just this. During the TM technique, the mind goes beyond the boundaries of routine to the unbounded field of creative intelligence. This sense of widened perception removes the frustration and brings freshness and enjoyment into life, even into routine, it is this sense that enables us to perceive more and more avenues of expression for our growing creativity—at work, at home, with our friends, and in the community.

What about society's problems — poverty, unemployment, and all those?

The TM program increases energy creativity and intelligence. With those three qualities we can solve all these other problems. More lively and creative people find their life continually improving: they're no longer in poverty, no longer unemployed. The nature of life — which is to progress and expand — takes over, and life becomes not a struggle, but a joy.

What's needed is to integrate creative thinking with constructive activity for the good of all.

What about mental health? I hear that one half of the hospital beds in the United States are taken by mental patients.

First, regular practice of the TM technique is excellent insurance against all diseases, including mental illness, as we've already discussed.

Further, the TM program shows remarkable potential in therapy of mental patients. It is very easy to do, easy to teach, and inexpensive. And it works! Many patients who haven't responded to any therapy show improvement with the TM technique.

A review of more than 100 studies shows the TM technique to be extremely effective for reducing anxiety, much more effective than the other methods tested.

Greater Reduction of Anxiety

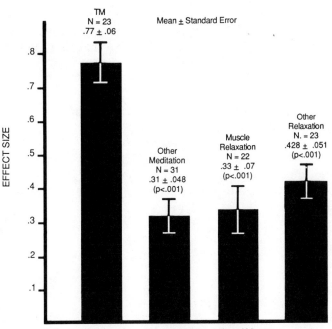

Studies matched for population and adjusted for duration, attrition and follow-up.
(p values are for compared comparisons between TM and other meditation and relaxation techniques)

REDUCTION OF TRAIT ANXIETY: A META-ANALYSIS

Through hand and computer searches of *Psychological Abstracts, Science Citation Index, Social Science Citation Index, Comprehensive Dissertation Index, Medline, Excerpta Medica,* and *Sociological Abstracts,* entries using the keywords "meditation" and "relaxation" were located. A meta-analysis was performed on the most commonly used measure, trait anxiety. Data was entered on a large number of variables such as population, experimental design, demand characteristics, experimenter's attitude, source of the study, duration, hours of treatment, attrition, pretest anxiety level, etc.

Effect sizes for Transcendental Meditation (TM), other forms of meditation (OM), muscular relaxation (MR), and other forms of relaxation (OR) were compared. TM had significantly (p<.001) larger effect size than the other groups, which were not significantly different among themselves. TM and MR were also compared to various subcatagories of OM and OR. TM was significantly superior to all the other techniques. MR was similar to all other (non-TM) treatments except for concentration meditation, which had significantly smaller effect size.

There were no significant differences for any of the groups between studies found in scientific journals, Ph.D. dissertations, or the unpublished TM archives. The difference between TM and the other groups was still significant if only studies published in journals were considered.

Reference: Kenneth Eppley, Allan Abrams, and Jonathan Shear, "Effects of Meditation and Relaxation on Trait Anxiety: A Meta-Analysis," (Paper presented at the August 1984 Convention of the American Psychological Association, Toronto, Canada), *Scientific Research on the Transcendental Meditation and TM-Sidhi Program: Collected Papers,* Vol. 4 ,in press, (MIU Press, 1985).

How about crime?

Crime is based on weakness. If someone has desires that he cannot fulfill lawfully, he is tempted to commit crimes. The TM program strengthens the mind while improving creativity and intelligence. It removes this basic weakness.

That sounds as if it would be useful for rehabilitation. Have prisoners tried TM?

Prisoners and prison staff, both. Tens of thousands of inmates and correctional officers in over 100 prisons throughout the world have learned the TM technique. Research on these inmates shows a wide spectrum of behavioral benefits.

One of the most important new studies shows a significant reduction in recidivism for prisoners who practice the TM program.

What is recidivism?

Recidivism is the "bounce-back" factor — how many inmates return to prison after release or parole, and how quickly. It can be used as an indicator of the success or failure of the rehabilitation provided by a prison or correctional institution. If the rehabilitation program were truly successful, no one would return. Over 60% of all inmates in maximum security prisons in the United States return to prison after parole. The cost to society — in lives, financial resources, and creativity — is astounding.

Reduced Criminal Recidivism

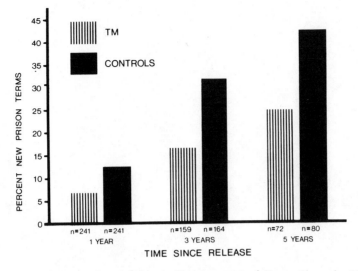

250 felons paroled from the California Department of Corrections in 1976 - 1982 showed substantially reduced recidivism after receiving TM instruction.

1) By comparison to a control group matched for parole year, institution, prior commitment record, age, race, and drug use history, the TM group had more clean records, more arrests or jail sentences under 90 days (considered by the California Department of Corrections as a relatively favorable outcome), and many fewer new prison terms at one through five years after release as determined from rap sheets ($p < .05$).

2) With other recidivism predictors (such as IQ, pre-TM prison rules violations, and participation in prison-sponsored education and psychotherapy) compensated for statistically, the TM group overall had about 25% new prison terms vs. 35% for the controls.

3) TM recidivists surveyed in prison while serving new terms or parole revocations were significantly ($p < .002$) less regular in meditation than the not-yet-released meditators.

4) Using data on lengths of new prison sentences, the TM group reduction in new prison terms with other predictors controlled can be extrapolated to estimate that TM reduced the mean length of new prison terms by 5.7 months per released meditator, including nonrecidivists. If we assume that only half of each sentence need be served, and allow a cost of $20,000 in direct and indirect costs per man-year in prison, the TM group as a whole (250 men) reduced their costs for new terms by about $1.2 million below costs for the controls. The prison TM program evaluated in this study was actually supported by the TM movement and by private donations. Given a TM fee of $800 per institutional client, this TM program for 250 clients would have cost only $200,000 had it been state supported, and would thus have been highly cost-effective.

Reference: Catherine R. Bleick and Allan I. Abrams, "The Transcendental Meditation Program and Criminal Recidivism in California," *Journal of Criminal Justice*, (Ann Arbor, Michigan, U.S.A., in press).

Autonomic Stability
Spontaneous Skin Resistance Responses

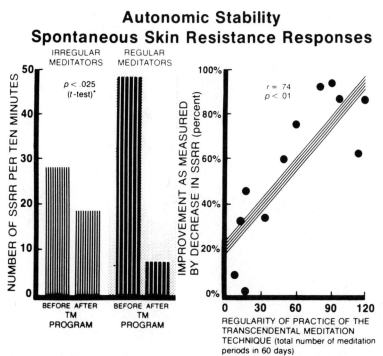

*Change in irregular —change in regular meditators

REHABILITATION OF PRISONERS I:
IMPROVED PHYSIOLOGY

Finding: The Transcendental Meditation technique reduced the level of stress in prisoners, as measured physiologically by number of spontaneous skin resistance responses (SSRR). The study showed that regular practice of the TM technique was positively correlated with the degree of increase in autonomic stability.

Interpretation: The Transcendental Meditation program is a truly effective means for rehabilitation, because it stabilizes the prisoner's physiology allowing him to direct his energies more positively and to assume more responsibility for his life.

Reference: David W. Orme-Johnson, John Kiehlbauch, Richard Moore, and John Bristol, "Personality and Autonomic Changes in Prisoners Practicing the Transcendental Meditation Technique," (La Tuna Federal Penitentiary, New Mexico, U.S.A.).

Rehabilitation of Prisoners II

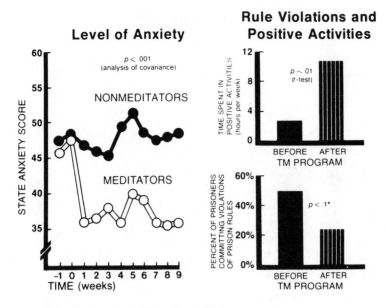

Level of Anxiety

Rule Violations and Positive Activities

* Mann-Whitney U test comparing meditators and nonmeditators.

REHABILITATION OF PRISONERS II:
IMPROVED SOCIAL BEHAVIOR

Finding: Three measures on prisoners practicing the Transcendental Meditation technique indicated:

1. a reduction in anxiety, as measured by the Spielberger State-Trait Anxiety Inventory (STAI)

2. a reduction in prison rule violations

3. an increase in time spent in positive activities

Interpretation: The Transcendental Meditation program produces the physiological and psychological normalization necessary for true and lasting rehabilitation.

First Reference: David Ballou, "The Transcendental Meditation Program at Stillwater Prison," (University of Kansas, Lawrence, Kansas, U.S.A.).

Second Reference: Monte Cunningham and Walter Koch, "The Transcendental Meditation Program and Rehabilitation: A Pilot Project at the Federal Correctional Institution at Lompoc, California."

Reduced Drug Abuse

Drug Use

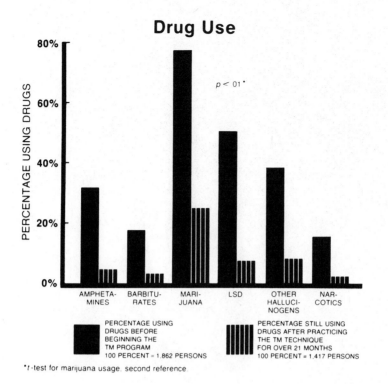

PERCENTAGE USING DRUGS

$p < 01$ *

| AMPHETA-MINES | BARBITU-RATES | MARI-JUANA | LSD | OTHER HALLUCI-NOGENS | NAR-COTICS |

PERCENTAGE USING DRUGS BEFORE BEGINNING THE TM PROGRAM
100 PERCENT = 1.862 PERSONS

PERCENTAGE STILL USING DRUGS AFTER PRACTICING THE TM TECHNIQUE FOR OVER 21 MONTHS
100 PERCENT = 1.417 PERSONS

*t-test for marijuana usage, second reference.

REDUCED DRUG ABUSE (USA)

Finding: A retrospective study of 1,862 subjects who practiced the Transcendental Meditation technique an average of 20 months showed decreases in the reported use of non-prescribed drugs.

Among the 852 subjects who had practiced the TM technique over 22 months, only 12.2% used marijuana, 3% used LSD, 4% used other hallucinogens, 1.2% used narcotics, 1.2% used amphetamines, and 1% used barbiturates. Nearly all these subjects who continued to use drugs reported using them only very rarely.

Interpretation: Because the Transcendental Meditation program improves inner control and decreases anxiety and strengthens mental health and general well-being, it may be concluded that the desire for drugs is thereby decreased or eliminated. This study indicates that the Transcendental Meditation program may be the most effective antidote for drug abuse, because its success does not depend on any initial resolve on the part of the subject to discontinue bad habits.

First Reference: Herbert Benson and Robert Keith Wallace, "Decreased Drug Abuse with Transcendental Meditation: A Study of 1,862 Subjects," *Drug Abuse: Proceedings of the International Conference,* ed., Chris J. D. Zarafonetis (Philadelphia, Pennsylvania, U.S.A.: Lea and Febiger, 1972): 369–376 and *Congressional Record,* Serial No. 92–1 (Washington, D.C., U.S.A.: Government Printing Office, 1971).

TM breaks the cycle of crime — prison — more crime...

Research at Walpole Prison in Massachusetts and at San Quentin and Folsom prisons in California evaluating the TM program found that three years after parole 30-40% fewer of the TM meditators were back in prison. That's a 30-40% decrease in recidivism among TM meditators. Since it costs the taxpayers between $10,000 and $20,000 a year to keep a person in prison, the savings have been enormous.

Millions and millions of dollars.

At least.

I've got one more question. Couldn't a person become a more creative criminal?

No. The strength to act correctly, in harmony with nature and society, and the clear perception of the practicality of right action grow as creativity grows. Regular contact, twice daily, with the unified field of all the laws of nature, transcendental consciousness, makes life-supporting behavior spontaneous.

Drug abuse?

People seem to take drugs for one of two reasons: either for fulfillment, which the TM program provides, or for escape, which the program eliminates the need for. The TM technique is deeply satisfying. The increased success in activity is also satisfying. Drug abuse seems to drop away because the desire for the drugs is gone.

A Prisoner at
Niedershönenfeld Prison
Germany

"For three years I was totally dependent on morphine. Then after breaking into a chemist's shop and being sent to prison I was forced to give up hard drugs.

"This did not mean that I no longer desired drugs; there was hardly a day when I did not think of the syringe, it just depended on my mood— sometimes more, sometimes less.

"The urge to use the syringe behind bars was much greater because I thought it would make me totally free.

"This is what I thought until I started the Transcendental Meditation program. I very soon discovered that my thoughts turned less towards drugs and today I don't even think about drugs at all. I am very happy about that. I know that man's desire for freedom can only be satisfied by meditation because meditation means to be free.

"I look forward to many more such insights."

G. LeDain, et al.
*Report of the Commission of Inquiry
  into the Non-Medicinal Use of Drugs*
21 January 1972
Canada

"Most of the respondents (61.1 percent) believed that the Transcendental Meditation program was extremely important in reducing or ending their drug use."

Paul Andrews
Project Director
Drug Education
Commonwealth of Massachusetts

"The TM program is without question a non-chemical alternative to drug abuse."

Melba Shepard
Executive Director
Boulder Youth Services

"We have had some experience with the Transcendental Meditation process and have found that it can be a factor in reduction of drug abuse."

What about alcohol and cigarettes?

Use of Alcohol and Cigarettes

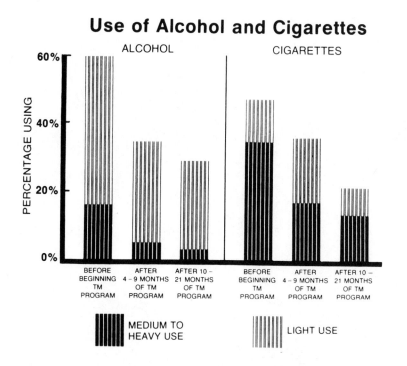

REDUCED USE OF ALCOHOL AND CIGARETTES

Finding: A retrospective study of 1,862 subjects who had practiced the Transcendental Meditation technique an average of 20 months showed a significant reduction in the reported use of alcohol and cigarettes.

Interpretation: The Transcendental Meditation technique has been shown to provide deep relaxation to the entire nervous system and to remove tensions, giving rise to a more calm, restful, and creative functioning of mind and body. These effects may be taken to explain the gradual decrease in the need for alcohol and cigarettes seen in this study.

Reference: Herbert Benson and Robert Keith Wallace, "Decreased Drug Abuse with Transcendental Meditation: A Study of 1,862 Subjects," *Drug Abuse: Proceedings of the International Conference,* ed. Chris J. D. Zarafonetis (Philadelphia, Pennsylvania, U.S.A.: Lea and Febiger, 1972): 369–376 and *Congressional Record,* Serial No. 92–1 (Washington, D.C., U.S.A.: Government Printing Office, 1971).

What about prejudice and bad feeling among groups of people?

There will always be different groups of people, different cultures, and different ways of life.

Problems arise when a narrow awareness and stress produce rigid boundaries among groups. The TM program develops appreciation and the ability to harmonize differences. Then these differences co-exist and can be appreciated for their own value.

Increased Tolerance in High School Students

Tolerance Scale
Jackson Personality Inventory

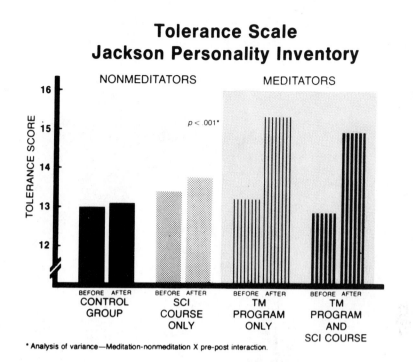

* Analysis of variance—Meditation-nonmeditation X pre-post interaction.

INCREASED TOLERANCE
IN HIGH SCHOOL STUDENTS

Finding: In a study of 80 students at a public high school in Canada, students who practiced the Transcendental Meditation technique showed a significant increase in tolerance ($p < .001$) after 14 weeks of the TM program, as measured by the Jackson Personality Inventory, whereas the control group did not. The increase in tolerance was shown to be primarily due to the effects of the practice of the TM technique itself, and not simply to intellectual involvement with the theory underlying it, as presented in an accompanying Science of Creative Intelligence course.

Interpretation: This finding has extremely important implications for the modern urban high school, which is attended by students from many different ethnic and social backgrounds. Increased tolerance may be seen as the natural result of the greater self-confidence, warmth, and positivity shown to be developed by the TM program. On a deeper level, increased tolerance reflects an expanded area of identification coming from deeper experience of the self. The Transcendental Meditation program promises secondary education a means to develop this quality in its students as part of the regular curriculum.

Reference: Howard Shecter, "The Transcendental Meditation Program in the Classroom: A Psychological Evaluation," (York University, North York, Ontario, Canada).

Aren't cultures being absorbed into one another?

At the moment, to a great extent, yes. It is essential that the individuals in each culture have greater stability so that they can hold on to the values of their culture while taking full advantage of the tremendous progress of our age. With the TM technique, each person develops his own nature, and this includes his own cultural nature, in a stable, integrated way. From this firm platform we can review the achievements of other cultures, and the demands of technology and changing times, and accept only those ideas which really support and help our growth.

The only way different cultures will be preserved is if those in each culture practice the TM program so that we can remain stable in the values of our culture and not be at the mercy of the winds of change.

What about the environment—ecology?

The thousands of individual problems that make up the basic problem of ecological balance all require more creativity and intelligence for their solution.

Equally important, these problems must be solved in such a way that they do not create worse problems. They must be solved with a breadth of awareness that takes in the entire situation, by minds that intuitively select the course of action that is completely life-supporting.

The TM program develops his breadth of awareness and this spontaneous knowledge of right action.

Johannes Olivegren
Professor of Architecture
Chalmers University of Technology
Sweden

"In many parts of the world much of the modern man-made environment is destroying the natural beauty of our landscapes, making urban life hectic and dangerous and our homes and working places impersonal and uninspiring. The TM program will open the eyes and inspire the creativity of planners, architects, builders, politicians, and laymen so that our houses, cities and landscapes will be a more life-supporting environmental frame for a rich and harmonious life for everybody."

Simon Cohen
Senior Probation Officer
Hampshire Probation Service
Hampshire, England

"As the TM program frees people to use more of their full potential, it deepens their awareness of other people and the world they live in. When people change in this way their social and political systems must follow."

And world peace?

World peace is a problem of individual peace. For a forest to be green all the trees must be green. For us to have world peace we must start with each individual becoming fulfilled. This is the only possible basis for lasting world peace. And it is a *real* basis.

Governmental and community leaders around the globe have praised and endorsed the promise of the Transcendental Meditation program to establish a stable, better world. An appeal to the governments of the world, made by Members of Parliament from all the States of India, puts it very beautifully:

> "Live in peace or perish is the challenge of the nuclear age. The state of increasing tension cannot continue indefinitely; it must give way to peace or annihilation . . . Maharishi's simple Transcendental Meditation program bridges the gulf between the inner and outer aspects of life. It regenerates the personality improving all phases of life, resulting in a harmonious development of body, mind, and soul. . . . It is our national duty to alleviate atmospheric tensions as soon as possible by eliminating the tensions in the lives of every individual. This can best be accomplished by giving the people a simple technique of creating powerful influences of peace and harmony from the deepest level of their consciousness—by a few minutes of daily practice of the Transcendental Meditation technique. . . . Increased consciousness means greater energy, creative intelligence, better health and also greater harmony in social relationships. Maharishi's simple Transcendental Meditation technique is a direct way to it. It is only necessary for us all to adopt it."

> Taken from the text of an appeal made by Members of Parliament from all the States of India, 1963.

That sounds pretty far-reaching. But how do you get everyone in the world to participate in the TM program?

We don't need to. All we need is one person in one hundred, and the whole of society will enjoy the benefits.

One in one hundred? How can so few make any difference?

It was once thought that any program to improve the quality of life of society as a whole would have to directly involve a majority of the population. For several years, researchers have been studying the wide range of benefits that the Transcendental Meditation program produces in every area of individual life: health, psychology, efficiency, and creativity. Recently, sociological studies of more than one hundred cities in the U.S.A. revealed a striking and important new phenomenon taking place.

Sociologists found that when only 1% of a population is practicing the Transcendental Meditation program, the whole population suddenly begins to measurably increase its efficiency, orderliness, and productivity. This is phase transition——

Phase transition?

"Phase transition" is a term from physics and chemistry. It refers to a basic change in the orderliness of any natural system. The change from a drop of water to a snowflake is one example of phase transition. The crystalline structure of the snowflake is far more orderly than the random arrangement of molecules when water is in the liquid state.

Scientists doing research on the TM technique have speculated that a somewhat similar phase transition takes place producing a more orderly functioning of the neurons of the brain. In the same way, the phase transition model may apply to basic changes in society. We can think of the overall effect of the TM program as bringing a change in society, from a chaotic state to a more harmonious one.

Best of all, research has shown that an improvement in the quality of life does not necessarily require everyone to practice the TM technique.

Because of the concentrated influence of orderliness and balance that the TM program produces, 1% of the population practicing the program is enough to maintain the coherent functioning of the entire society.

This phase transition that begins when 1% is meditating was predicted on the basis of the natural laws in physics and other sciences and has now been borne out by a comprehensive survey of scores of cities in which 1% are practicing the TM program. For example, in matched *non* meditating cities the crime rate increased 7.7% in one year, but in cities reaching the 1% transition point the crime rate fell an average of 8.8%—a net improvement of nearly 17%.

228

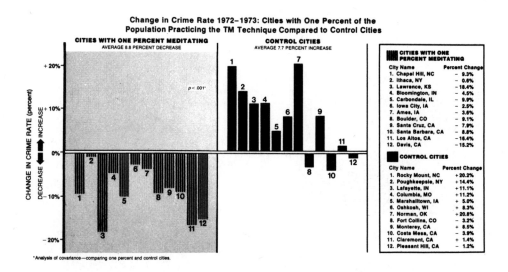

Change in Crime Rate 1972–1973: Cities with One Percent of the
Population Practicing the TM Technique Compared to Control Cities

DECREASED CRIME IN THE ENVIRONMENT OF INCREASING CRIME IMPROVED QUALITY OF CITY LIFE

Finding: This retrospective study compared 12 cities in which at least one percent of the population had learned the Transcendental Meditation technique by the end of 1972 to 12 matched control cities with relatively few people practicing the TM technique but otherwise comparable in population, location, and crime statistics. Nine of the 12 control cities increased in number of serious crimes from 1972 to 1973 with an average change of +7.7 percent. According to the FBI Uniform Crime Reports for the nation as a whole, the average increase in crime that year in cities of comparable size was 8.7 percent. In contrast, the cities with one percent of their population practicing the TM technique decreased in crime rate by an average of 8.8 percent, a relative decrease of 16.5 percent when compared with the control group.

This difference in change in crime rate between the two groups of cities was statistically significant (p <.001, analysis of co-variance). Furthermore, the correlation between percentage of meditators and decrease in crime rate for cities in this sample was 0.66 (p <.001), a statistically significant degree of correlation.

Interpretation: Any sociological study has many uncontrolled variables, making it difficult to prove definitely a relationship of cause and effect. In this case, however, the effect seen is consistent over many cities. Furthermore, the many dramatically proven effects of improved orderliness of physiology and psychology and improved interpersonal relationships seen in individuals practicing the Transcendental Meditation technique suggest that a group of individuals practicing the technique cannot help but influence the quality of life of the whole population. Increased harmony and balance in an individual's behavior naturally increase harmony and balance in the life of the city. This initial survey indicates that one percent of a city's population practicing the TM technique is sufficient to bring about a noticeable transformation in the quality of life.

Reference: Candace Borland and Garland Landrith III, "Influence of the Transcendental Meditation Program on Crime Rate in Cities," (Maharishi International University, Fairfield, Iowa, U.S.A.).

229

The fact that the crime rate drops so significantly in most 1% TM cities shows that the positive influence of the people practicing the Transcendental Meditation program reaches all the way through the fabric of society. Think how much *more* effect this increased orderliness must have on people who are already involved in constructive and useful behavior for the good of society!

Hundreds of research programs around the world have verified the beneficial effects of the Transcendental Meditation program in individual life. Now an important breakthrough in the field of sociology has revealed the capability of the program to enable us to solve the age-old problems of mankind in this generation.

This research establishes that a person practicing the TM technique has so profound an influence on his surroundings that any community, city, state, or nation can easily reach phase transition in a few weeks or months. And after the transition point is achieved, increasing progress and improvement of society are both spontaneous and inevitable.

Chapter 6

Unified Field Based
Ideal Civilization

I can see that all these effects of the TM program would make our life much better, but why do you say "Unified Field Based Ideal Civilization?"

In the last 300 years society has progressed from the industrial age to the space age and the computer age. Each new age has been the result of some great new scientific discovery of deeper, more powerful levels of nature's functioning and the technological application of these discoveries for the benefit of society. The most recent discoveries suggest still more promising technologies. The great possibilities we have been discussing through the TM technique are actually based on the discovery of the deepest, most profound level of nature's functioning, the unified field of all the laws of nature. Life based on this technology is what we call Unified Field Based Ideal Civilization.

What will that be like?

Maharishi has described it, saying, "Society will be characterized by harmony and dynamic progress. Education will be ideal, producing fully developed citizens. Health will be perfect. Every culture will be enlivened and its integrity will be strengthened. The achievements of every government will be enhanced. Nations will rise to invincibility. Nature will be balanced — the seasons will come on time, crops will be abundant, there will be no natural catastrophes. There will be peace in the family of nations. The whole world will live in the full sunshine of the Age of Enlightenment."

That sounds wonderful, but could you start by telling me what exactly *is* the unified field?

The unified field is a term scientists use to describe the most fundamental level of the universe, the unified source of the infinite energy, intelligence, creativity and organizing power displayed in nature. Albert Einstein spent the final years of his life searching for this field. Today modern physicists have succeeded in gaining a glimpse of the unified field through various unified field theories and supporting research.

A glimpse?

Yes, a glimpse. And the fascinating thing is that the more scientists discover about the unified field, the more their description matches the description given by Vedic science.

233

What is Vedic science?

Vedic science is the complete science of life, unfolding full knowledge of the knower, the process of knowing, and the object of knowledge.

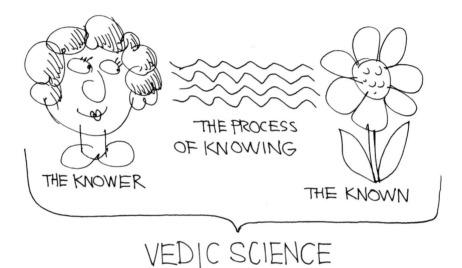

It comes from the most ancient and continuous record of human experience known to mankind. As brought to light by Maharishi, Vedic science provides a complete description of the unified field and the technology for anyone to apply this field to daily living.

Slower, please. First tell me more about the unified field.

Much of our recent scientific and technological progress has been based on locating four main forces in nature, forces which govern the entire universe. They are the electromagnetic force; the weak force and the strong force, which bind together the nucleus of the atom; and the gravitational force. Application of these four forces has brought great progress and comfort to society. Electric generators, computers, satellites, atomic energy — these technologies are the direct result of the application of the four fundamental forces.

In the last few years, a series of theoretical and experimental breakthroughs by physicists point to one unified field that underlies the four forces of nature. It also unifies these force fields with the matter fields that structure elementary particles, the building blocks of nature.

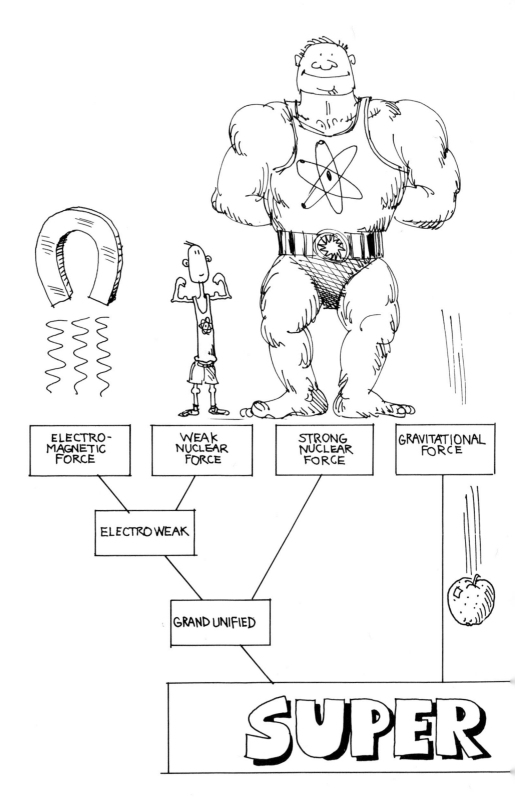

ELECTRO-
MAGNETIC
FORCE

WEAK
NUCLEAR
FORCE

STRONG
NUCLEAR
FORCE

GRAVITATIONAL
FORCE

ELECTRO WEAK

GRAND UNIFIED

SUPER

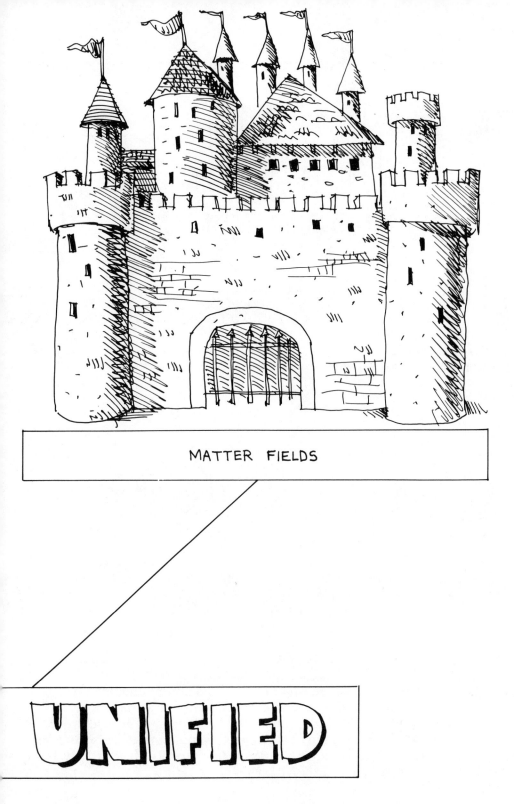

MATTER FIELDS

UNIFIED

Discovery of the Unified Field of Natural Law by Modern Science

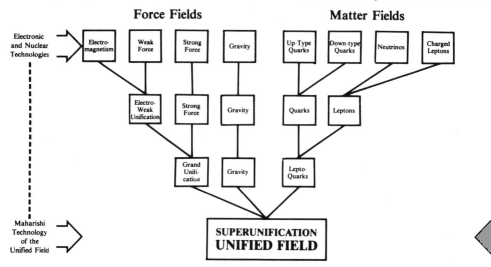

Quantum physicists propose the unification of all force and matter fields of nature through the principle of supersymmetry. Transcendental Meditation allows the conscious mind to identify itself with the

Why don't we leave this discussion to the physicists?

Because it has very practical applications to us in our daily life. One of the most exciting recent breakthroughs is the discovery that the unified field interacts with itself to produce all of these building blocks of creation. This quality of self-interaction or self-referral means that the unified field has the ability to create from within itself.

And?

According to Vedic science this self-referral level of nature's functioning is a field of pure, transcendental consciousness, which can be directly experienced by any human being through the TM program. This field of least excitation of consciousness is experienced as pure awareness being aware of itself. That means, in practical terms, that the infinite creativity, dynamism and organizing power of nature is lively within us.

238

Experience of the Unified Field of Natural Law
through Transcendental Meditation

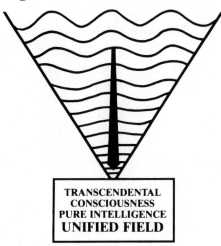

unified field of all the laws of nature in transcendental consciousness, thereby enlivening all the beautiful evolutionary qualities of the unified field in individual thought and action.

Would you explain a little bit more about the unified field and self-referral?

Self-referral means that the unified field refers back to itself for knowledge, for information, for organizing power. All the knowledge for the creation, maintenance and evolution of the universe is contained within the unified field. The unified field creates everything from within itself. It doesn't require anything outside of itself to create the universe.

In some ways the self-referral activity of the unified field is like the relationship between an airplane and the control tower. The plane's flight is directed by the control tower. The pilot refers back to the control tower for precise information and directions that are appropriate for his flight conditions.

We can call this "tower referral". The pilot refers to the tower and the tower directs the activity of the plane.

In this example, the plane and the tower are separate, but this is not so in the case of the unified field. The unified field is located at the deepest level of nature's functioning. It is self-sufficient and creates the entire universe from within itself. It is the source of the individual and all of his actions. When we practice the TM and TM-Sidhi program, we as individuals refer back to the unified field and identify our conscious awareness with its own source, the unified field of all the laws of nature. This is how we fully align ourselves with the total potential of natural law, and have all of nature's organizing power to spontaneously guide our thought, speech and action.

One more time. Could you repeat the whole thing?

Certainly. According to Vedic science, the deepest level of objective nature, the unified field, and the deepest level of human nature, transcendental consciousness, are not different; they are the same. In other words, my essential nature, your essential nature and nature's essential nature are identical. They are all the unified field.

What's the unified field like?

Because the unified field is the fountainhead of natural law, all the qualities in the universe have their origin in the unified field. A few key characteristics of this most fundamental level where consciousness and matter are unified are...

SELF-REFERRAL

INFINITE SILENCE

UNBOUNDEDNESS
TOTAL POTENTIAL OF NATURAL LAW

PURE KNOWLEDGE
SELF-SUFFICIENCY

INFINITE CORRELATION

INVINCIBILITY

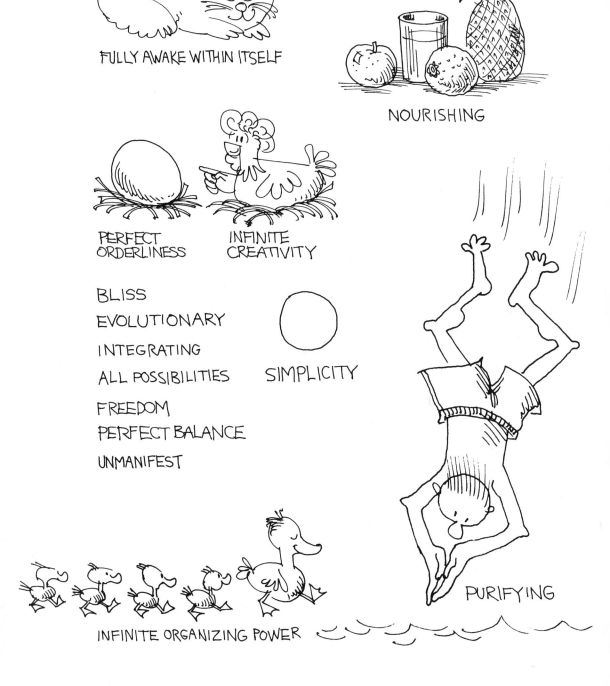

FULLY AWAKE WITHIN ITSELF

NOURISHING

PERFECT ORDERLINESS

INFINITE CREATIVITY

BLISS
EVOLUTIONARY
INTEGRATING
ALL POSSIBILITIES
FREEDOM
PERFECT BALANCE
UNMANIFEST

SIMPLICITY

PURIFYING

INFINITE ORGANIZING POWER

INFINITE DYNAMISM

IMMORTALITY

How does modern science relate to Vedic science?

The objective knowledge provided by modern science provides one part of Vedic science, the knowledge of the known. Vedic science also includes knowledge of the knower (subjective knowledge), as well as knowledge of the link or relationship between the knower and what is known. These three branches of knowledge support and enrich each other. Together they provide knowledge of the whole of life.

Can you tell me more about how transcendental consciousness fits into this?

Transcendental consciousness is consciousness in its least excited state. This most quiet level of our own awareness is the perfectly silent, settled, unbounded level of consciousness before it rises up into thought and action, like a silent ocean before it rises up in waves. At this deepest level of life, consciousness and the unified field are the same.

But how do I know that the state of least excitation of consciousness is the unified field of natural law?

Excellent question. Besides the scientific theories we've been discussing, there are three other ways. When you sit to practice the TM technique you directly experience the least excited state of consciousness as that unbounded, silent, yet infinitely dynamic unified field of all laws of nature. This direct experience is the first verification.

And?

Your experience is validated by the scientifically measurable effects that the TM and TM-Sidhi programs have on the individual, society and the world.

And?

These can be verified by referring to time-honored texts, such as Vedic literature, which provide the oldest records of human experience.

What does all this mean to me?

It means that the qualities of the unified field are the qualities of your own essential nature, consciousness in its least excited state. If your awareness is identified with this deepest level of life, you can spontaneously enliven and display the infinite creativity, intelligence and organizing power of nature in your own daily life.

What's the practical value?

Functioning from the unified field, we can live in perfect harmony with nature. We don't make mistakes, we don't suffer in life. We grow in the direction of perfect health, happiness, and fulfillment.

The unified field contains the total potential of natural law. It is responsible for the creation and continued existence of everything — you, your family, our earth, the whole universe. It's like the central computer that administers all the enormous variety of things going on all over everywhere all the time in nature. If you can think and act from there, you have all the infinite organizing power of nature working with you. This is what the Maharishi Technology of the Unified Field makes possible for you.

TIME FOR THE ECLIPSE

MAKE SURE THE APPLES RIPEN

LOOK IN ON THE CATERPILLARS
TO MAKE SURE THEY BECOME BUTTERFLIES

BRING SPRING

PATCH UP THE OZONE LAYER

KEEP THE SKY BLUE

KEEP WARM AIR RISING

CONTINUE GRAVITY

RENEW WIND

RE CHARGE ELECTROMAGNETISM

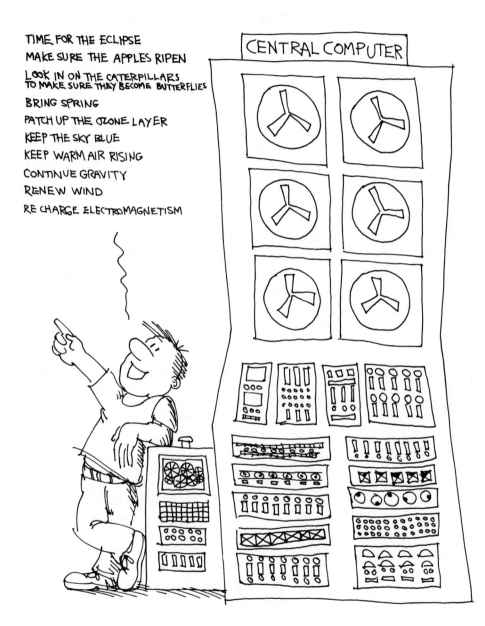

CENTRAL COMPUTER

Maharishi Technology of the Unified Field? What's that?

TM is a part of it.

I understand about that, but is there more? I've heard about the TM-City program — what's that?

Not "City", but Sidhi!

Oh, well then, what's the TM-Sidhi program?

As we said earlier, the TM technique allows the mind to experience the state of least excitation of consciousness, the unified field of all the laws of nature. The TM-Sidhi program makes this field functional.

Functional ?

Yes. It is an advanced program that develops our natural ability to operate from that deepest level of our own self, the unified field. We learn to directly enliven the unified field for ourselves and the world.

And ?

We call the TM-Sidhi program "research into consciousness as a field of all possibilities" because we learn to enliven and develop the latent, unused potential of the mind and body.

For example?

Sidhi means "perfection". Through the TM-Sidhi program we systematically and scientifically develop perfection in the functioning of the nervous system, the brain, and the senses, as well as culture the finest values of the heart and emotions.

CENTRAL COMPUTER

SURFACE LEVEL
OF THE SELF

DEEPEST
LEVEL
OF THE
SELF

START

This I can understand, but what's this "yogic flying" I keep hearing about? Is that really part of the TM-Sidhi program?

Yes. The TM-Sidhi program improves mind-body co-ordination and "yogic flying" is the result of perfect mind body co-ordination.

Mind-body co-ordination?

You know — you have the thought to stand up and you stand up. That's mind-body co-ordination.

In the TM-Sidhi program we learn to function from the state of least excitation of consciousness which is the unified field of all the laws of nature. By perfecting mind-body co-ordination from that all-powerful level of nature's functioning, we learn to operate from that level of all possibilities so that if we have a thought for the body to lift up, the body lifts up.

254

Is anyone really flying?!

Yes, the first stage. There are three stages predicted for "yogic flying." The first stage is described as "hopping." In this stage it is common for the body to lift up and move forward a few feet. The second stage is described as a "hovering" or floating. The third stage is described as "movement through air." Tens of thousands of people all over the world — doctors, lawyers, housewives, business people — are enjoying short hops. This first stage of "yogic flying" is accompanied by an inner experience of great bliss and striking changes in how the mind and body are functioning.

Is this really natural?

Yes. The TM-Sidhi program is as simple, natural, and effortless as the TM technique, and nothing could be simpler than that. Psychologists estimate that we use about 5% of our potential. The TM-Sidhi program speeds the development of the other 95% of our normal capabilities.

What about criminals learning the TM-Sidhi program! Couldn't they use these powers to be super criminals?

No. The TM-Sidhi program develops the sidhis based on contact with the unified field of *all* the laws of nature. When one functions from this level it's not possible to do anything that violates the law or harms one's self or others. Instead, one develops all the evolutionary qualities of the unified field.

What's the value of all this?

The deepest value is the full development of consciousness, and we know that full development of consciousness is at the basis of success in life. We are able to fulfill all our desires quickly, completely and spontaneously without any harm to ourselves or our surroundings. That is perfect alliance with natural law.

Regular practice of the Maharishi Technology of the Unified Field develops an enlightened individual — an enlightened mother, an enlightened dentist, an enlightened student, an enlightened electrician, an enlightened musician, an enlightened carpenter, an enlightened anyone.

"Enlightened" means?

"Enlightened" means we live the absolute *full* potential of our life in perfect alliance with natural law.

Alliance with natural law? What does that mean?

As we know, the entire universe is governed by laws of nature. The vast movements of the galaxies, the motions of the electrons, and all of life go on according to specific laws of nature.

The unified field described by Vedic science, and glimpsed by modern science, is the ground state of all the laws of nature, and the source of the infinite organizing power of nature. During the TM technique the individual mind identifies with the unified field. During the TM-Sidhi program we learn to make the unified field functional.

This way, we function from the unified field with every thought we think and every action that we perform — whether writing an essay for school, caring for our family, playing baseball or balancing our checkbook. Anything we do, we do with the infinite organizing power and support of nature.

What do you mean by support of nature?

Have you ever had a day when everything just seemed to be going right?

Yes...

Like those times when you really need a parking place and just as you drive up, a car pulls out from the spot in front of you and you think, "Ah, my lucky day!"?

Or the person you've been unable to reach on the telephone for days calls you up "out of the blue"? Or those days when everyone you need to see and everything you need to do just falls into place?

Yes, I've experienced that. I wish it would happen more often. Do you call that support of nature?

Yes. When we live spontaneously in alliance with natural law; when every thought, word and action is spontaneously right and helpful to our surroundings, then we find that nature supports our lives in return. Our desires are spontaneously fulfilled.

There is a law in physics that says for every action there is an equal and opposite reaction.

So we find that our life becomes spontaneously easier, smoother, more productive and more evolutionary when we attune ourselves with natural law through the TM and TM-Sidhi program. It's very real and very fulfilling. Life ceases to be a struggle. Through support of nature life is bliss.

Support of Nature

Could you explain the research that supports all this?

As we discussed earlier, with the Maharishi Technology of the Unified Field — the TM and TM-Sidhi program — we unfold our full mental potential. From a physiological standpoint, that would have to mean optimizing brain functioning.

Optimizing brain functioning? What's that?

Good question. Using the full potential of the mind would have to imply using the full potential of the brain. According to neurophysiologists, different parts of the brain have different functions. For example, the front of the brain is associated with memory, creativity, and higher moral reasoning. The back of the the brain is associated with vision, and other perceptions. In addition, the brain has two hemispheres. Scientists feel that the functioning of one hemisphere may be associated with rational or analytical thinking, and the other with spatial or intuitive thinking. Recently they have shown that even the simplest activities are associated with rapidly changing complex patterns of brain activity.

While there is integration between different parts of the brain in order to walk, speak, and do the things we do, the different areas of the brain are not working as closely together as they might.

How can you know that?

One way is to study brain waves with EEG.

EEG?

EEG stands for electroencephalography, and measures the electrical energy generated by billions of nerve cells in the brain. By studying the EEG of the brain, a neurophysiologist can determine whether a person is awake, dreaming or sleeping — or whether he is experiencing transcendental conciousness, the state of least excitation of consciousness.

You mean the TM practice produces different brain waves than waking, dreaming or sleeping?

Absolutely. The unique physiological and biochemical style of functioning produces unique brain waves as well.

And what happens to EEG?

During the experience of transcendental consciousness, the brain wave patterns from the activity in different parts of the brain are far more similar. This indicates a profound orderliness of functioning of the brain. It means the different parts of the brain are working together as a coherent whole. This we call "optimizing brain functioning".

261

Here, let's have a look at some research. The "mountain peaks" you see on the next charts are taken from a sophisticated computer analysis and represent periods of high coherence in brain functioning.

Growth of EEG Coherence
with the Growth of Enlightenment

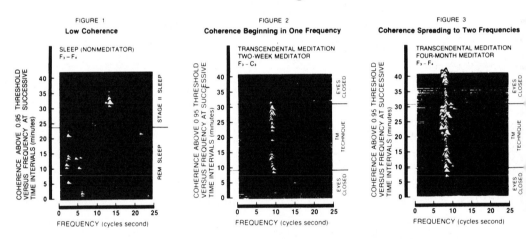

Measurements of orderliness or coherence in brain functioning can be made by computer analysis of the EEG signals from two or more different parts of the brain. These displays show coherence above a threshold of 95% of perfect coherence, plotted in axes of frequency and time. In sleep there is very little coherence (fig.1). However, during the initial periods of practicing the Transcendental Meditation technique, high coherence begins the moment the technique is commenced (fig.2). After regular practice of Transcendental Meditation, coherence spreads to several frequencies, including those associated with activity, and persists after meditation as a permanent feature of physiological functioning (fig.3-5). This coherence is correlated with speed of physiological recovery, high creativity, and the subjective experience of higher states of consciousness. These characteristics of enlightenment are developed more rapidly and completely through the TM-Sidhi program (fig.6).

The last frame of the chart shows brain wave coherence generated during the TM-Sidhi program. According to the research, the TM-Sidhi program, particularly the technique for flying, greatly optimizes brain functioning. This means the whole brain works together to accomplish the goal. Actually, it's the brain wave coherence that produces the specific TM-Sidhi effect, like flying.

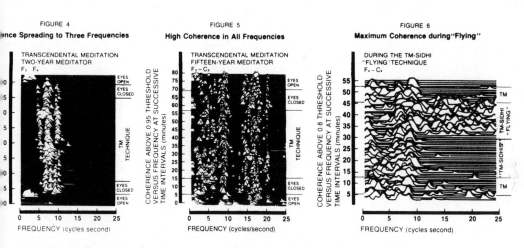

FIGURE 4

nce Spreading to Three Frequencies

TRANSCENDENTAL MEDITATION
TWO-YEAR MEDITATOR
F₃ F₄

FREQUENCY (cycles second)

FIGURE 5

High Coherence in All Frequencies

TRANSCENDENTAL MEDITATION
FIFTEEN-YEAR MEDITATOR
F₃ – C₃

COHERENCE ABOVE 0.95 THRESHOLD
VERSUS FREQUENCY AT SUCCESSIVE
TIME INTERVALS (minutes)

FREQUENCY (cycles/second)

FIGURE 6

Maximum Coherence during "Flying"

DURING THE TM-SIDHI
"FLYING" TECHNIQUE
F₄ – C₄

COHERENCE ABOVE 0.8 THRESHOLD
VERSUS FREQUENCY AT SUCCESSIVE
TIME INTERVALS (minutes)

FREQUENCY (cycles second)

First Reference: Paul H. Levine, J. Russell Hebert, and Christopher T. Haynes, "EEG Coherence during the Transcendental Meditation Technique" (MERU, 1975). Published in *Scientific Research on the Transcendental Meditation Program: Collected Papers*, Volume I. West Germany, MERU Press, 1976.

Second Reference: David W. Orme-Johnson, Geoffrey Clements, Christopher T. Haynes, and Keredine Badaoui, "Higher States of Consciousness: EEG Coherence, Creativity, and Experiences of the Sidhis" (MERU, 1977). Published in *Scientific Research on the Transcendental Meditation Program: Collected Papers*, Volume I, 2nd edition. West Germany, MERU Press, 1977.

Third Reference: D.W. Orme-Johnson, R.K. Wallace, M.C. Dillbeck, E. Lukenbach, and N.A. Rosenberg, "Recent Biochemical and Physiological Research on the Transcendental Meditation and TM-Sidhi Program: Clinical and Epidemiological Applications." Paper presented at the American Psychiatric Association, Chicago, June 1979.

Optimizing Brain Functioning through the Tra

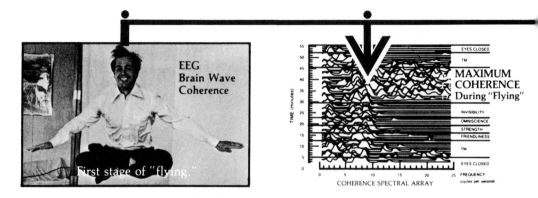

EEG
Brain Wave
Coherence

First stage of "flying."

MAXIMUM
COHERENCE
During "Flying"

EYES CLOSED
TM
INVISIBILITY
OMNISCIENCE
STRENGTH
FRIENDLINESS
TM
EYES CLOSED

TIME (minutes)

COHERENCE SPECTRAL ARRAY

FREQUENCY
(cycles per second)

Optimum brain functioning, as indicated by maximim coherence (orderliness) in brain wave activity during the TM-Sidhi practice, creates the perfect conditions for the frictionless flow of awareness towards the fulfillment of its desire. The principle of least action, which governs all activity in nature and uses the skill of nature to quietly accomplish everything, is available in its optimum value when brain wave coherence is maximum and awareness is in its simplest state.

In the flying technique, at the moment of maximum coherence, the body lifts up and begins to hop (the first stage of flying). Simultaneously, the subjective experience is one of waves of exhilaration. In this way the flying technique accelerates evolution to enlightenment — the state of fulfillment free from suffering and problems.

The TM-Sidhi program marks the most exciting breakthrough in thirty years of global research into conciousness through the TM program. A natural extension of the TM technique, the TM-Sidhi program is an even more advanced technology of higher consciousness.

The TM technique locates the silence within the activity of the mind: it systematically gives the experience of the least excited state of consciousness, pure consciousness, as a profoundly blissful field, but static, unmoving.

Pure consciousness is the ground state of human awareness. Because laws of nature are impulses of consciousness, pure consciousness is also the home of all the laws of nature. An impulse originating from this level becomes an impulse of nature itself. Here is a technology whereby each life-supporting desire irresistibly finds fulfillment because it automatically enjoys the support of all the laws of nature. Pure consciousness thus becomes the natural focal point from which to influence nature. The TM-Sidhi program is really a technology for learning to think and act from the simplest state of awareness, where thought and action are most natural and therefore most evolutionary. This is the natural mechanics of human capability in its highest form: creating outward achievement purely by inward, effortless activity, the unmanifest activity within the field of one's own awareness. Through the TM-Sidhi program, the life of the individual becomes a life of all possibilities — man becomes master of creation.

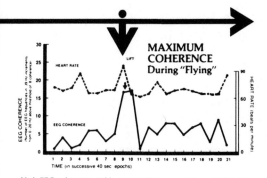

MAXIMUM COHERENCE During "Flying"

High EEG coherence and heart rate during experience of "flying"

> Maximum coherence in brain waves accomplishes the specific ability. In the case of the "flying" ability, the body lifts up at the point of maximum coherence.

Moreover, consciousness is naturally a field of correlation, and pure consciousness is the field of infinite correlation. The ability to be active within pure consciousness creates a profoundly coherent influence that radiates out from the individual into the environment, enlivening all the laws of nature for the enrichment and evolution of life everywhere. The TM-Sidhi program is thus the most powerful technology ever discovered for individuals to enrich the harmony and promote the progress of their society to the fullest.

How does "yogic flying" work?

As we've just seen, the TM and TM-Sidhi program produces a unique ordering or coherence in brain functioning. EEG research on "yogic flying" has shown that the body lifts up at the moment of maximum EEG coherence.

What's the experience like?

During the TM technique the mind experiences a state of "restful alertness" during which the awareness is deeply settled, yet fully awake. During the "yogic flying" technique, one experiences waves of exhilaration and a profound stabilization of this silent level of awareness.

But why demonstrate "yogic flying" now?

Because "yogic flying" provides a powerful demonstration that the subjective and objective fields of life do arise from one unified field, and that by enlivening that field as the most settled state of our own awareness we can create an influence of coherence, harmony and positivity for the whole world. We'll look at how this works in detail on pages 290-308.

Eddie Gob and Blaine Watson

People Weekly, July 28, 1986

Photo by Stanley Tretick **People Weekly**© July 28, 1986 Time, Inc.

Sounds like fun.

Absolutely. On July 9, 1986 the First North American Yogic Flying Competition was held at the Washington, D.C. Convention Center.

FIRST NORTH AMERICAN YOGIC FLYING COMPETITION

WORLD RECORDS, JULY 9, 1986, WASHINGTON, DC

50-meter dash 23.33 seconds, Eddie Gob, Guadeloupe
25-meter hurdles 11.53 seconds, Eddie Gob, Guadeloupe
Long jump 70 inches, Eddie Gob, Guadeloupe
High jump 24.75 inches, Blaine Watson, Canada
High jump 27.00 inches, So Kam Tim, Hong Kong:
   MIU, Fairfield, Iowa, August 29, 1986

CHRONOLOGICAL AGE   BIOLOGICAL AGE

Is there any other new research?

Yes. There is now considerable research showing that the TM and TM-Sidhi programs can actually slow or reverse the aging process.

Reverse aging? By doing what, changing my birth certificate!

No, the deep rest actually makes your body younger! There is a difference between chronological age, which is the age of your body in years, and biological age, which can be understood as the age of your body in wear and tear.

Insurance companies have developed a standardized medical exam to distinguish a person's actual biological age from their chronological age.

You mean a 40-year old could have a 25-year old body?

Exactly. The first scientific research on the long-term practice of the Maharishi Technology of the Unified Field and effects on biological aging was conducted by Dr. Robert Keith Wallace in 1982. He found that for people practicing the TM program for less than 5 years, their biological age was an average of 5 years younger than their chronological age. The TM subjects who had been practicing more than 5 years averaged 12 years younger. Four subjects had biological ages 27 or more years younger than their chronological age.

Reduction of Biological Age

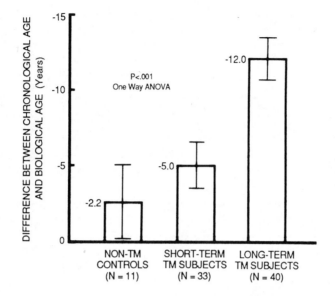

A standardized test of biological age, the Adult Growth Examination, was given to a cross-sectional group of men and women with a mean age of 53 years. They were divided into three groups: nonmeditating controls, short-term TM meditators (under five years) and long-term TM meditators (over five years). The average biological age of the nonmeditating controls was 2.6 years younger than their chronological age; of the short-term meditators, 5.0 years younger than their chronological age; of the long-term meditators, 12.0 years younger. A statistically significant difference was found between the long-term meditators and both the control group and short-term meditators ($F = 8.05$, $p < .001$, one-way ANOVA). Further, a significant correlation ($r = .46$, $p < .001$) was found between younger biological age and length of time practicing the TM technique.

These findings suggest that practice of the TM technique slows or reverses the aging process — and that the longer one practices the TM technique, the younger his biological age when compared with his chronological age. The deep rest experienced during the TM technique allows the physiology to dissolve stress. As a result, mind and body become more stable, adaptable, and integrated — less susceptible to wear and tear — and the aging process is reduced and reversed.

Reference: R. Keith Wallace, Eliha Jacobe, and Beth Harrington, " The Effects of the Transcendental Meditation and TM-Sidhi Program on the Aging Process." *International Journal of Neuroscience*, 16 (1) 1982: 53-58.

This study, taken together with the 350 other scientific research studies on the Maharishi Technology of the Unified Field, makes it easy to see why Maharishi says this technology develops perfect health and longevity.

Scientific research indicating the reversal of aging t

PHYSIOLOGY

	Usual Changes with age	Improvements with the TM and TM-Sidhi program
Blood pressure — systolic	↑	↓
Blood pressure — diastolic	↑	↓
Cardiovascular efficiency	↓	↑
Cerebral blood flow	↓	↑
Vital capacity	↓	↑
Maximum voluntary ventilation	↓	↑
Auditory threshold	↑	↓
Auditory discrimination	↓	↑
Near point of vision (accommodation)	↑	↓
Homeostatic recovery	↓	↑
EEG alpha power	↓	↑

BIOCHEMISTRY*

Serum cholesterol concentration	↑	↓
Hemoglobin concentration	↓	↑

PSYCHOLOGY

Susceptibility to stress	↑	↓
Behavioral rigidity	↑	↓
Learning ability (paired associate learning)	↓	↑
Memory — (short term)	↓	↑

*A small number of changes resulting from the Transcendental Meditation and TM-Sidhi program are not directly opposite to the changes produced by aging. These changes are nevertheless important. For instance, cortisol levels and metabolic rate decrease with Transcendental Meditation and with aging. The changes occurring with aging are related to the accumulated loss of tissue as a result of general wear and tear, whereas the changes occuring with Transcendental Meditation are associated with decreased stress levels and greater efficiency of metabolic processes.

PSYCHOLOGY continued

	Usual changes with age	Improvements with the TM and TM-Sidhi program
Memory — (long term)	⬇	⬆
Organization of memory	⬇	⬆
Creativity	⬇	⬆
Abstract reasoning	⬇	⬆
Intelligence	⬇	⬆
Dichotic listening	⬇	⬆

MIND-BODY COORDINATION

	Usual changes with age	Improvements with the TM and TM-Sidhi program
Reaction time	⬆	⬇
Sensory-motor performance (Mirror Star-Tracing Test)	⬇	⬆

HEALTH

	Usual changes with age	Improvements with the TM and TM-Sidhi program
Cardiovascular disease	⬆	⬇
Hypertension	⬆	⬇
Asthma (severity)	⬆	⬇
Immune system efficiency	⬇	⬆
Sleep disturbance (arousals/night)	⬆	⬇
Insomnia and insufficient sleep	⬆	⬇
Daytime sleep	⬆	⬇
Quality of sleep	⬇	⬆
Depression	⬆	⬇

All these factors show deterioration with the aging process. The opposite changes — indicating a reversal of the aging process — are observed with the Transcendental Meditation and TM-Sidhi program.

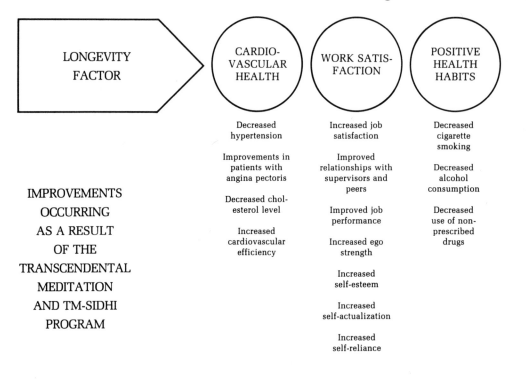

LONGEVITY FACTOR

CARDIO-VASCULAR HEALTH

WORK SATIS-FACTION

POSITIVE HEALTH HABITS

IMPROVEMENTS

OCCURRING

AS A RESULT

OF THE

TRANSCENDENTAL

MEDITATION

AND TM-SIDHI

PROGRAM

Decreased hypertension

Improvements in patients with angina pectoris

Decreased cholesterol level

Increased cardiovascular efficiency

Increased job satisfaction

Improved relationships with supervisors and peers

Improved job performance

Increased ego strength

Increased self-esteem

Increased self-actualization

Increased self-reliance

Decreased cigarette smoking

Decreased alcohol consumption

Decreased use of non-prescribed drugs

The eight factors shown above have been found to be most clearly showing improvements in all these areas indicate the stabilization o dental Meditation and TM-Sidhi program.

The first seven factors shown above in order of importance were identified by a major study (E. Palmore, 1974. Norm been found to be of great importance for longevity and good health in later life (G.E. Valliant, *New England Journal o*

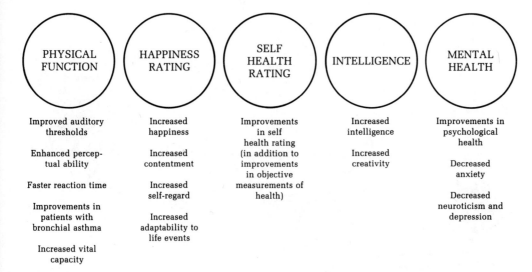

PHYSICAL FUNCTION	HAPPINESS RATING	SELF HEALTH RATING	INTELLIGENCE	MENTAL HEALTH
Improved auditory thresholds	Increased happiness	Improvements in self health rating (in addition to improvements in objective measurements of health)	Increased intelligence	Improvements in psychological health
Enhanced perceptual ability	Increased contentment		Increased creativity	Decreased anxiety
Faster reaction time	Increased self-regard			Decreased neuroticism and depression
Improvements in patients with bronchial asthma	Increased adaptability to life events			
Increased vital capacity				
Improved running speed and agility				
Improved perceptual-motor performance				
Reduced inflammation				
Relief from insomnia				
Faster recovery from stress				
Improved bio-chemical stability, homeostasis, and efficiency				
Reduced cortisol (a major stress hormone)				
Restful style of physiological functioning				

related to longevity. The research results listed beneath each factor,
perfect health and the promotion of longevity through the Transcen-

ing II, Durham: Duke University Press. U.S.A.) to be closely related to longevity. The last factor, mental health, has
dicine, 1979, 301,1249-1254).

How does the TM program produce all these changes in the direction of longer life?

By restoring balance of the mind, body, behavior and environment and reconnecting them with the underlying field of natural law. This is called the balancing principle. Balance can be brought to life from the side of the mind, with TM, and also from the side of the body, behavior and environment. A branch of Vedic science, Ayurveda, provides knowledge and procedures for restoring balance. In fact, TM is Maharishi Ayurveda's approach to health from the angle of consciousness.

Ayurveda? Maharishi Ayurveda?

"Ayu" means life or lifespan. "Veda" means science — systematic, repeatable knowledge. So Ayurveda is the science of life, the science of very long life. Ayurveda, which comes from the heritage of India, is the oldest system of medicine in the world. It emphasizes prevention. Due to foreign influences in India and fascination with modern medicine Ayurveda had been neglected even in India, but now Maharishi, working with the ancient texts and the world's leading Ayurvedic physicians, has restored it to its completeness. Complete Ayurveda is called Maharishi Ayurveda and is fully effective in the preservation of health and the elimination of illness.

According to this completely natural system of health care, aging and illness are the result of imbalance and lack of harmony among the many factors that make up our mind, body and environment. When harmony is restored using the balancing principle of Maharishi Ayurveda, then the ground for disease is eliminated.

Tell me more!

The underlying goal of Maharishi Ayurveda is very profound — a perfect health, long life and enlightenment for every individual. We know from modern physics that all matter, including our own bodies, is the expression of the unified field of natural law, and we know from Vedic science that the unified field is consciousness in its pure state. Maharishi Ayurveda assures that all the qualities of the unified field, such as self-sufficiency, infinite organizing power, perfect balance, dynamism and immortality, are vital in our lives so that we live a long life, grow in perfect health and immortality, and rise to the state of enlightenment.

How does Maharishi Ayurveda promote health?

There are a variety of time-tested procedures tailored to the individual's constitution or body type. Maharishi Ayurveda recognizes that people are different. A diet, food supplement or treatment which is good for one person may not be useful for someone else. Maharishi Ayurveda has a very detailed understanding of individual differences and the first thing that the doctor at the Maharishi Ayurveda Medical Center does is to identify what is called the individual constitutional type. Once you know what type you are it is easy to tailor the daily and seasonal routine, diet, exercise and food supplements that are best for maintaining good health, strengthening the immune system, promoting longevity and maintaining the greatest vitality of body and mind.

Treatments for illness are holistic, natural and without harmful side-effects. Rather than primarily treating symptoms, Maharishi Ayurveda treats disease at its source and actually eliminates the ground for disease. Many illnesses which are chronic or difficult to treat can be helped through Maharishi Ayurveda. Most importantly, an individual can gain proper understanding of what to do each day to prevent illness and actually grow to perfect health.

Has research been done on Ayurveda?

Hundreds of scientific studies on Ayurveda have been conducted world-wide. Research on the Maharishi Ayurveda Medical Programs has shown that the benefits of Maharishi Ayurveda include increased energy and vitality, increased positivity and balance of emotions, signs of rejuvenation, accelerated reversal of aging, improved digestion and sleep patterns, improved mental clarity, strengthened immune system and increased happiness.

Where can I find out more about Maharishi Ayurveda?

You can get more information and take advantage of these programs at the Maharishi Ayurveda Medical Centers in major cities throughout the world. These centers have been established by leading medical doctors and the foremost Ayurvedic physicians, working under the guidance and inspiration of Maharishi. They have developed programs for the preservation of health, the promotion of longevity, the prevention of illness and the treatment of disease. In addition, your own doctor can consult with the world's leading Ayurvedic physicians through the International Consultation Service of the Maharishi World Center for Ayurveda, India.

The development of Maharishi Ayurveda is in response to the world-wide requirement for effective, low cost, natural health care. As part of a global Campaign to Create a Disease-free Society, Maharishi Ayurveda Medical Centers have been established in many nations around the world. This is an essential part of Maharishi's program to create world peace because individual and collective good health is essential for peace among the family of nations.

What causes disease and suffering in the first place?

Sickness and suffering are the result of violation of natural law. One obvious example is, we eat something wrong and we fall sick. Violating natural law causes stress; and stress, doctors say, is the cause of 80-90% of all illness. In addition, the overwhelming buildup of stress, by billions of people in the world constantly violating the laws of nature in their thoughts and actions, causes outbreaks of collective disasters, like social, economic and natural upheavals.

But why are people always violating natural law?

Simple. Educational systems throughout the world fail to educate or train each person to function from the unified field of all the laws of nature. Only from this level is it possible to spontaneously think and act in perfect alliance with all the laws of nature.

Any solution?

Yes, adding the Maharishi Technology of the Unified Field to the daily routine of classes.

How does that work?

It's called the Maharishi Unified Field Based Integrated System of Education, and it is used in schools and universities in over 20 countries. In the USA this system has been in use for over 15 years at MIU.

What is MIU?

MIU stands for Maharishi International University. MIU was founded in 1971 by Maharishi to accomplish these goals.

Seven Goals

1. To develop the full potential of the individual

2. To improve governmental achievements

3. To realize the highest ideal of education

4. To eliminate the age-old problem of crime and all behavior that brings unhappiness to the family of man

5. To maximize the intelligent use of the environment

6. To bring fulfillment to the economic aspirations of individuals and society

7. To achieve the spiritual goals of mankind in this generation

---

The main campus of the university was established in 1974 in Fairfield, Iowa. In 1980 MIU was granted accreditation by the North Central Association of Colleges and Schools. MIU, like other great universities, has top caliber faculty and academic excellence in the traditional disciplines.

As of January, 1986, accredited programs include B.S. and B.A. degrees in Physics, Chemistry, Mathematics, Biology, Psychology, Education, Art, Literature, Computer Science, and Electronic Engineering, Business Administration, and Government; masters degrees in Computer Science, Business Administration, Education, Higher Education Administration, Professional Writing, Science of Creative Intelligence, and Fine Art; and Ph.D. degrees in Administration, the Neuroscience of Human Consciousness, Physiology, Psychology and Physics.

But what makes MIU special?

As we said, at MIU the traditional disciplines have been integrated with the TM technology. With the Maharishi Unified Field Based Integrated System of Education, all academic disciplines from physics and mathematics to literature and the arts are taught from the perspective of the unified field which underlies all expressions of the universe and therefore all branches of knowledge. MIU integrates the strengths of traditional education with the knowledge and experience of the unified field of all the laws of nature.

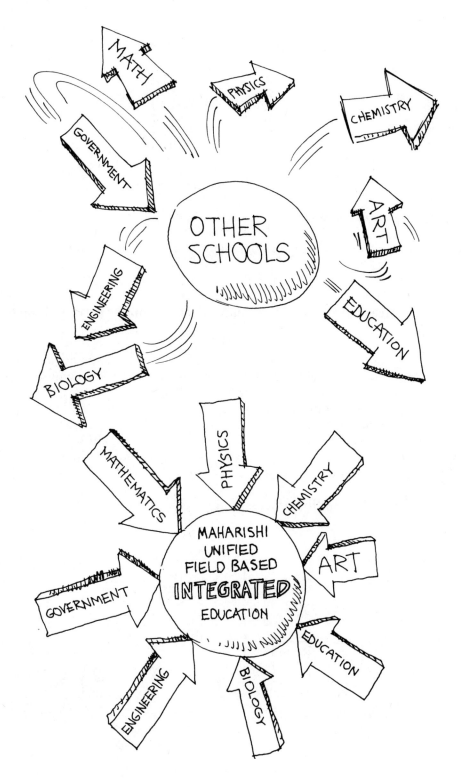

What does that accomplish?

A fully educated man or woman. It prevents fragmentation. You've heard of the "knowledge explosion?"

Yes, what is learned today in a graduate physics seminar may be obsolete in a year.

Or even six months. The MIU curriculum offers the most recent advances of knowledge in all the disciplines, taught in the light of their common basis in the unified field. And twice a day the student directly experiences the unified field in the simplest form of his awareness through the Maharishi Technology of the Unified Field. This way, the student becomes a specialist in his field, while at the same time he owns the basis of *all* knowledge in his awareness. He learns to own the whole tree of knowledge at its source, as well as the branches and leaves.

But, most important to this process of integration is...

PURE CONSCIOUSNESS — THE UNIFIED FIELD

Is?

Everyone on campus is an expert in the Maharishi Technology of the Unified Field — students, faculty, administration, staff — everyone.

Everyone practicing the Maharishi Technology of the Unified Field! It must be amazing...

Like no place on earth. By contacting and enlivening the unified field in their awareness twice a day through the Maharishi Technology of the Unified Field, the students can directly relate the theoretical knowledge of the unified field gained during their studies with their own direct experience of the unified field gained during their practice of the TM and TM-Sidhi program. Students learn to function in perfect alliance with all the laws of nature. Learning becomes fun, challenging, exciting — and relevant.

Actually, it's like heaven on earth. The feeling on campus and in the town is so vital, fresh and alive, and yet it is so harmonious and stress-free. It is the perfect environment to learn, to create, to raise a family, to grow in enlightenment — to become educated. It really is an ideal society — and well worth seeing for yourself!

That sounds good! But how do MIU students rank academically?

Exceptionally well. MIU has a very liberal admissions policy, yet graduates score well above the national average on competence tests in their fields. Many more MIU undergraduates go to graduate school than the national average, and they excel at the best schools. And at the MIU School, grades K-12, students, on the whole, consistently score in the top 1% of all students in the nation on standard national tests of academic performance.

And how do MIU graduates fare after college?

Alumni report a high level of satisfaction with their educational experience and with their preparation for success in professional and adult life. MIU graduates distinguish themselves in their careers. The creativity, vitality and discipline structured at MIU gives them a real competitive edge and prepares them for major success.

And the marvelous thing is that because the Maharishi Unified Field Based Integrated System of Education can be used in any school or university, without the need to revise the existing curriculum, all these achievements can belong to anyone, anywhere.

I have a different question. You've talked about the effects of this technology on the environment and the world. How can a person practicing the TM and TM-Sidhi program actually influence someone 100 miles away or in another part of the world? Is it possible?

Absolutely.

How?

To understand this we have to know a little about quantum field theory and the field effects of consciousness...

Wait a minute! First, what's a field?

I'll give you an example. A magnet has a field. We don't see it, but it's there and it holds up a note on the refrigerator door. Electromagnetism is a field. We don't see it, but it's there and your favorite television programs are broadcast through it.

A field is an unseen but very real level in nature that connects and communicates information at a distance from one object to another through waves. Follow me?

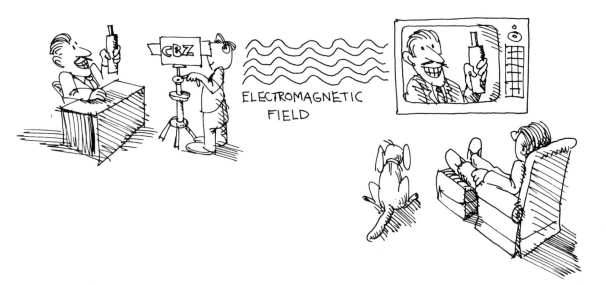

ELECTROMAGNETIC
FIELD

I follow what you're saying, but I'm still having difficulty picturing it.

Okay. Consider two corks floating on a pond. Push one cork down and waves spread out on the surface of the pond and soon the other cork is bobbing up and down.

In this analogy, the pond is the field and the waves passing through the field send information — or an influence — from one object to another.

That seems clear.

Good. Let's go on to the next point and use the example of light. You are familiar with laser light?

Well, I've heard of laser surgery and laser discs.

Right. Well, light is just waves, or excitations of the electromagnetic field. Laser light is far more intense than ordinary light. Why? Simply because all of the light waves in the beam are coherent. Instead of interfering with each other and cancelling each other out, it's as if they are all marching in step with one another. Coherent light is vastly more powerful than ordinary incoherent light. A laser on earth can cast a beam of light on the moon, but an ordinary bulb without reflectors and special lenses can only light a room or a building.

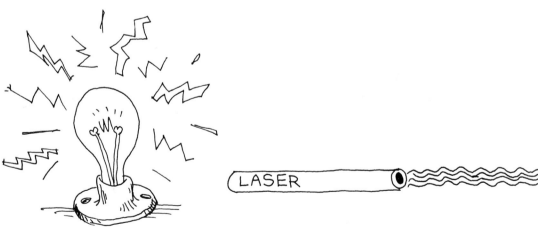

ORDINARY LIGHTBULB

Why is that?

A fundamental law of nature governing the behavior of fields states that any time a number of individual waves are coherent, then the combined intensity of the effect is proportional to the square of the number, or n^2.

That means, for example, if there are 100 incoherent light waves, then their intensity is proportional to 100 light waves. But, if they are coherent with one another, then their intensity is proportional to 100^2 or 10,000 light waves.

This is the difference between coherent light and ordinary light. Coherent light can be generated with lasers through the process of superradiance in which all the atoms emit their light in step with each other.

What does this have to do with the Maharishi Technology of the Unified Field?

Same principle. Experts in the Maharishi Technology of the Unified Field, practicing the program together in a group, enliven the unified field in a very powerful way. The unified field is the home of all the laws of nature; and when the unified field is enlivened, then all the laws of nature "wake up." With this enlivening of the unified field, a powerful influence of coherence and orderliness is radiated throughout the environment and the world.

You mean that if we do the TM and TM-Sidhi program in a group it's even more powerful than if we do it by ourselves?

Yes. The life-supporting effect for ourselves and others is multiplied hundreds, even thousands, of times.

Is there any scientific evidence demonstrating these effects?

Yes, over 30 major studies. The first was the 1974 crime study we mentioned before. Scientists compared 11 cities in the United States having more than 1% of the population practicing the TM program with 11 matched cities with less than 1% TM meditators. The results were clear: the 1% cities had an average 16% lower crime rate than the cities without 1% TM meditators. The decrease in crime came when the 1% threshold was reached.

On the basis of this research, Maharishi proclaimed on January 12th, 1975, "Through the window of science we see the Dawn of the Age of Enlightenment."

This study has now been replicated in hundreds of cities throughout the world using the most sophisticated statistical techniques and sociological controls.

Scientists researching this phenomenon called it the Maharishi Effect after Maharishi, who had first predicted it in 1960.

Scientists later predicted that since the group TM-Sidhi program is more powerful because it takes advantage of the superradiance effect in nature, a much smaller percentage — about the square root of 1% of a population practicing the TM-Sidhi program together — should be enough to improve all aspects of society.

In the summer of 1978 Maharishi inaugurated the Ideal Society Campaign with experts in the Maharishi Technology of the Unified Field practicing the TM-Sidhi program in small groups in 108 states and provinces throughout the world. Research showed a broad spectrum of changes in the quality of life in these test areas. Scientists termed this the "Extended Maharishi Effect".

Quality of life? What do you mean by that?

The scientists predicted many changes including reduced traffic accidents, reduced hospital admissions and improved economic conditions.

And the findings?

Improved Quality of Life

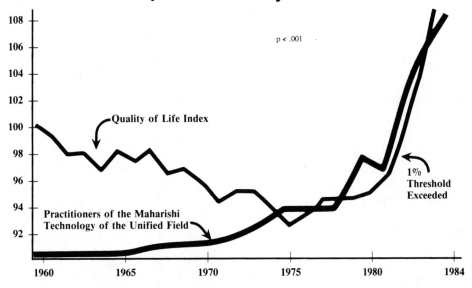

The quality of life in the United States as measured by an index comprised of 12 variables (crime rate, percentage of civil cases reaching trial, infectious diseases rate, infant mortality rate, cigarette and alcohol consumption rate, GNP per capita, patent application rate, degrees conferred rate, divorce rate, traffic fatalities rate, and hospital admissions rate) was found to decrease almost constantly from 1960 to 1975. In 1975 and 1976 several 100,000's of people were instructed in the Transcendental Meditation technique, bringing the rate over .4% in 1976. Cross correlation showed that the rate of practitioners of the TM technique had a leading relationship on the development of the quality of life. Since 1976, the quality of life has been improving continously, and the improvement started to accelerate sharply, once the 1% threshold — based on the combined effect of the number of meditators and the people engaged in the collective practice of the TM-Sidhi program at MIU, Fairfield — was exceeded in 1982, 1983 and 1984. The rate of improvement in Iowa, MIU's home state, has been significantly higher in these years.

The highly significant correlations (p<.0001) between the development of the quality of life and the proportion of people engaged in the Transcendental Meditation and TM-Sidhi program suggest that the practice of the Maharishi Technology of the Unified Field induces coherence throughout all levels of society, leading to improvements of all aspects of life. The temporal and spatial trends support this causal relationship strongly. Predictions on basis of the regression model indicate that the quality of life would improve tenfold every 4 years once a group of 7000 experts of the Maharishi Technology of the Unified Field would be established in the United States.

Reference: David W. Orme-Johnson and Paul Gelderloos, "The Long-Term Effects of the Maharishi Technology of the Unified Field on the Quality of Life in the United States (1960-1983). Updated version. (Department of Psychology, Maharishi International University, USA 1984). *Scientific Research on the Transcendental Meditation and TM-Sidhi Program: Collected Papers*, Vol. 4, in press, (MIU Press, 1985).

What about entire nations — nations at war?

The Extended Maharishi Effect was tested at a national level in the fall of 1978 during the World Peace Project. Teams of experts in the Maharishi Technology of the Unified Field were positioned in the five greatest trouble spots in the world — Nicaragua, Iran, Israel, southeast Asia and Rhodesia. The findings were unquestionable. Violence was calmed and peace returned to these areas for the few months of this project.

How?

As the United Nations Charter observes, wars begin in the minds of men. Changing the trends of the last thousands of years depends on changing trends of thinking from stress and struggle to success, progress and bliss. This happens naturally with the TM and TM-Sidhi program. Coherently functioning human brain physiology is the unit of world peace.

Increased International Harmony

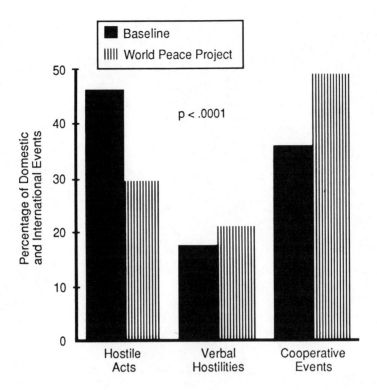

During a ten-week World Peace Project (October 8 - December 23, 1978) a total of 1,400 experts in the Transcendental Meditation and TM-Sidhi techniques went in groups to the world's five major trouble-spot areas in order to test the hypothesis that the group practice of this technology would create coherence in a field of collective consciousness, thereby restoring balance to the socio-political systems in those areas and in the world.

Evaluation of the project in the trouble-spot countries using a large independent data source on international conflict, the Conflict and Peace Data Bank (COPDAB) file, indicated that there was a significant proportional decrease of Hostile Acts and an increase of Cooperative Events in domestic affairs and international relations during this period compared with the preceding ten-week baseline period (chi-square = 18.51, p<.0001). By using the prior ten years as a control, this analysis showed that the results could not be attributed to weekly, monthly, or yearly cycles or to variability in the size of the weekly data sets.

Reference: David W. Orme-Johnson, Charles N. Alexander, and Jean G. Bousquet, "Impact Assessment Analysis of the Effects of Coherence Creating Groups on International Conflicts," (Department of Psychology, Maharishi International University, USA, 1985) *Scientific Research on the Transcendental Meditation and TM-Sidhi Program: Collected Papers*, Vol. 4, in press, (MIU Press, 1985).

Explain in more detail, please.

War is the outbreak of the built-up stress created by the violation of the laws of nature by the individuals in society. World peace can never be attained unless the stress is eliminated on the level of the individuals. Practice of the Maharishi Technology of the Unified Field, the TM and TM-Sidhi program, by the square root of 1% of the world's population in one place produces a powerful influence of coherence in world consciousness which neutralizes stress and promotes coherence and positivity in the whole population.

How?

As we explained before, on the level of the unified field, everything in the universe is connected. Since ancient times, the unified field has been described by Vedic Science as the field of pure transcendental consciousness, which can be located at the most silent level of human awareness.

The Maharishi Technology of the Unified Field is the technology of consciousness which allows an individual to directly *experience* the unified field during the TM technique and allows him to *enliven* the unified field during the TM-Sidhi program.

The TM and TM-Sidhi program creates coherence in brain functioning. An impulse of coherence generated at the level of the unified field during the practice of the TM-Sidhi program spreads throughout nature, creating a powerful influence of coherence on the collective consciousness of the entire population, neutralizing the negative tendencies and strengthening positive trends in society.

Why is now such a crucial time to demonstrate "yogic flying"?

Governments have failed to create world peace. Today, with the onset of terrorism, they have not provided safety to the people in any part of the world.

As Maharishi has said: "With the rising wave of terrorism and the dangerous rivalry of the superpowers, it is vital to immediately create an indomitable influence of coherence in world consciousness. The group practice of the Maharishi Technology of the Unified Field will make peace on earth powerful and power on earth peaceful. Coherence in world consciousness is the basis of world peace."

Has it ever been tried on a global level?

That was the grand experiment. Scientists theorized that about 7000 experts practicing the Maharishi Technology of the Unified Field together in one spot could generate an orderly influence of peace and prosperity for the entire world.

Why 7000?

7000 is approximately the square root of 1% of the population of the world. The Maharishi Effect predicts that 7000 should be sufficient to generate a positive influence of coherence and harmony in the whole world.

THE MAHARISHI TECHNOLOGY OF THE UNIFIED FIELD

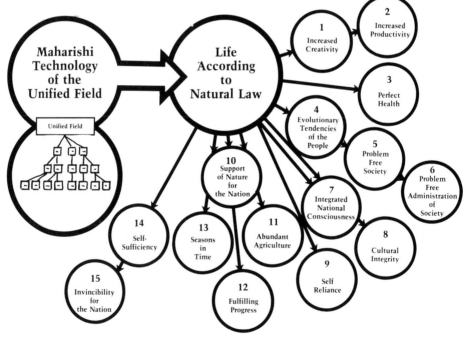

Full Sunshine of the Age of Enlightenment for Everyone and Every Nation

298

And the grand experiment?

From December 17, 1983 to January 6, 1984 at Maharishi International University in Fairfield, Iowa, a global Taste of Utopia Assembly was held: 7000 experts in the Maharishi Technology of the Unified Field assembled at MIU from 50 countries to give the world a "sample taste of utopia." In early December, before the conference, research scientists at MIU predicted that the reality of the global Taste of Utopia would be evidenced by improved relations between nations, greater cooperation between political parties, increased social harmony, and signs of worldwide economic recovery; and reflected in growing optimism, confidence and self-reliance, and a general sense of well-being in the family of nations.

Asked about the anticipated results, Maharishi said, "Anything that is good will rise; anything that is not good will vanish, as darkness disappears with the first ray of light."

And the results?

See for yourself. This the scientists termed the "Global Maharishi Effect."

Scientific Research on the Global Maharishi Effect

Taste of Utopia Assembly
December 17, 1983 — January 6, 1984
Maharishi International University
USA

7000 Experts in the Maharishi Technology of the Unified Field
Creating a Taste of Utopia for All Mankind

NUMBER OF EXPERTS IN THE MAHARISHI TECHNOLOGY OF THE UNIFIED FIELD

Beginning on December 17, the size of the coherence creating group at MIU increased to over 6855, the square root of one percent of the world's population. *On January 6, the Taste of Utopia Assembly ended and the number of experts participating in the collective performance of the Maharishi Technology of the Unified Field fell far below the number needed to maintain coherence and positivity in world consciousness.*

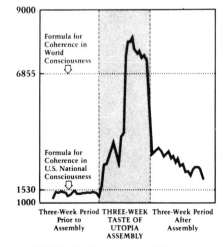

SOURCE: Capital of the Age of Enlightenment

INCREASED POSITIVITY OF EVENTS IN SITUATIONS OF INTERNATIONAL CONFLICT
Percent of Total Events as Rated for Degree of Conflict

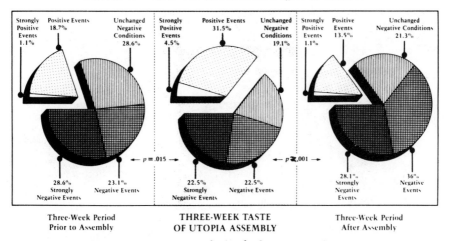

Three-Week Period
Prior to Assembly

**THREE-WEEK TASTE
OF UTOPIA ASSEMBLY**

Three-Week Period
After Assembly

SOURCE: Content Analysis of *The New York Times*

During the three-week period of the Taste of Utopia Assembly the balance of negativity to positivity in events pertaining to international conflicts in the trouble-spot areas of the world shifted significantly towards increased positivity. *After the Assembly the balance of events reverted towards increased negativity.*

INCREASED VITALITY AND POSITIVITY OF HEADS OF STATE
Percent of Events with Prior Negative Trends Rated for Reversal or Non-Reversal of Trend

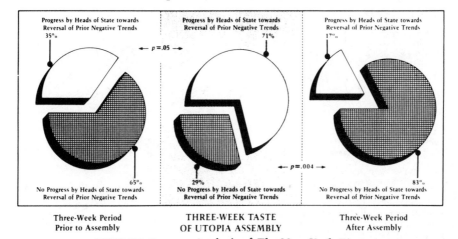

Three-Week Period
Prior to Assembly

**THREE-WEEK TASTE
OF UTOPIA ASSEMBLY**

Three-Week Period
After Assembly

SOURCE: Content Analysis of *The New York Times*

According to Maharishi's Absolute Theory of Government, government is the innocent mirror of the nation, and the head of state reflects by his speech and actions the quality of national consciousness. During the Taste of Utopia Assembly coherence increased in world consciousness as exhibited by more positive, evolutionary statements and actions of heads of state of nations throughout the world and by more national and international support for their policies and leadership. *After the Assembly the quality of the statements and actions of heads of state and of the support they received reverted towards less positivity.*

301

INCREASED POSITIVITY OF EVENTS IN LEBANESE CONFLICT
Percent of Total Events as Rated for Degree of Conflict

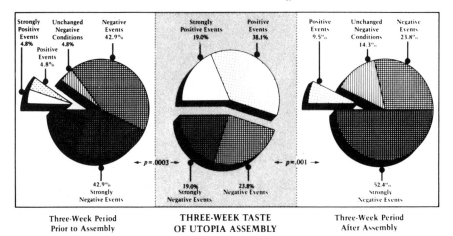

Strongly Positive Events 4.8%
Unchanged Negative Conditions 4.8%
Negative Events 42.9%
Positive Events 4.8%

Strongly Positive Events 19.0%
Positive Events 38.1%

Positive Events 9.5%
Unchanged Negative Conditions 14.3%
Negative Events 23.8%

← p = .0003 →   ← p = .001 →

42.9% Strongly Negative Events

19.0% Strongly Negative Events   23.8% Negative Events

52.4% Strongly Negative Events

Three-Week Period Prior to Assembly

THREE-WEEK TASTE OF UTOPIA ASSEMBLY

Three-Week Period After Assembly

SOURCE: Content Analysis of *An-Nahar* (Major Lebanese Newspaper)

During the three-week period of the Taste of Utopia Assembly positivity of events in Lebanon substantially increased, seen as progress towards peaceful resolution of the conflict. *After the Assembly the situation quickly deteriorated.*

(Note: The content analysis was conducted by a team comprising members of various interest groups in Lebanon.)

DECREASED INCIDENCE OF INFECTIOUS DISEASES

Percent Change in Total Incidence of Notifiable Infectious Diseases Compared to Medians for Equivalent Periods in Previous Years

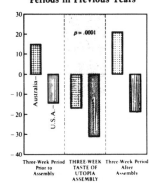

p = .0001

Three-Week Period Prior to Assembly

THREE-WEEK TASTE OF UTOPIA ASSEMBLY

Three-Week Period After Assembly

SOURCES: Center for Disease Control, U.S.A.; Department of Health, Commonwealth of Australia. (Note: Number of previous years considered—4 years for Australia; 5 years for U.S.A.)

The incidence of all major categories of notifiable infectious diseases decreased during the Taste of Utopia Assembly. *After the Taste of Utopia Assembly the incidence of infectious diseases began to rise again towards levels comparable to previous years.*

302

RISING WORLD STOCK INDEX
World Index of Capital International S.A., Geneva

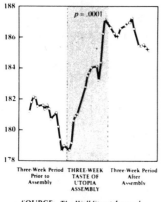

Three-Week Period Prior to Assembly	THREE-WEEK TASTE OF UTOPIA ASSEMBLY	Three-Week Period After Assembly

SOURCE: *The Wall Street Journal*

During the Taste of Utopia Assembly rising coherence from MIU created a wave of confidence and optimism throughout the world, seen as a rise in the World index, a composite of stocks from 19 countries. *After the Assembly the index resumed a downward trend.*

SIMULTANEOUS INCREASE OF MAJOR STOCK MARKET INDICES
Percent Change over Three-Week Period

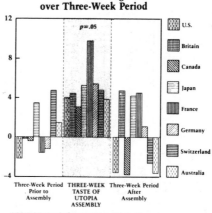

U.S.
Britain
Canada
Japan
France
Germany
Switzerland
Australia

Three-Week Period Prior to Assembly	THREE-WEEK TASTE OF UTOPIA ASSEMBLY	Three-Week Period After Assembly

SOURCE: Capital International S.A., Geneva (*Wall Street Journal*)

During the Taste of Utopia Assembly the major stock markets of the world increased simultaneously, indicating balanced economic growth world-wide. *After the Assembly the same major stock markets reverted to a pattern similar to that seen prior to the Assembly, with some increasing and some decreasing.*

REDUCED
CRIME TOTALS
Percent Change in Daily or Weekly Crime Totals

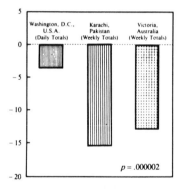

SOURCES: City Police Department, Washington, D.C.; Inspector-General of Police, Government of Sind, Karachi, Islamic Republic of Pakistan; Research and Development Department, Victoria Police, Melbourne, Australia.

Using time series analysis it was found that during the Taste of Utopia Assembly significant decreases occurred in daily or weekly crime totals, in locations on three continents, in comparison with the average daily or weekly totals for the 24 weeks prior to and three weeks after the Assembly.

INCREASED
PATENT APPLICATIONS
Percent Change in the Actual Number of Patent Applications Compared to Predicted Number

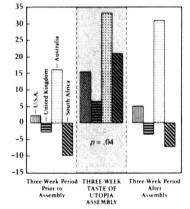

SOURCES: U.S. Patent Office; U.K. Patent Office; Australia Patent, Trade Marks, and Design Office; Government Patent Office, South Africa

During the Taste of Utopia Assembly the number of patents filed, an important measure of national creativity, increased significantly in countries on four continents. *After the Assembly the number of applications tended to revert to a pattern similar to that seen prior to the Assembly.*

DECREASED TRAFFIC FATALITIES
Percent Decrease in Traffic Fatalities, 17 December 1983 to 6 January 1984, Compared with the Number Predicted from Prior Years

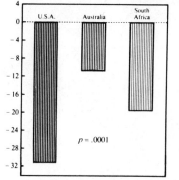

p = .0001

SOURCES: National Safety Council, U.S.A.; National Road Safety Council, South Africa; State Police Dept., Sydney, Police Dept., Perth, and Road Traffic Authority, Hawthorn, Australia.
(Note: Traffic fatalities for Australia are for Western Australia, New South Wales, and Victoria.)

Traffic fatalities decreased significantly during the Taste of Utopia Assembly. In the U.S.A., traffic fatalities per day over the Christmas and New Year's weekends were at an all-time low, even though miles driven per day, despite the cold weather, were at an all-time high.

WORLDWIDE DECREASE IN AIR TRAFFIC FATALITIES
Number of Air Traffic Fatalities From 17 December to 6 January

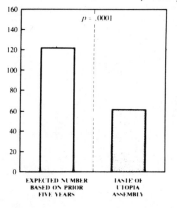

p = .0001

SOURCES: International Civil Aviation Organization; National Transportation Safety Board, U.S.A.

During the Taste of Utopia Assembly the number of air traffic fatalities in the world was 49% lower than the expected number based on the prior five years for the same time of year. It was also 29% lower than the lowest number during the equivalent three-week period in the prior five years.

Reduction of the War in Lebanon — 1984

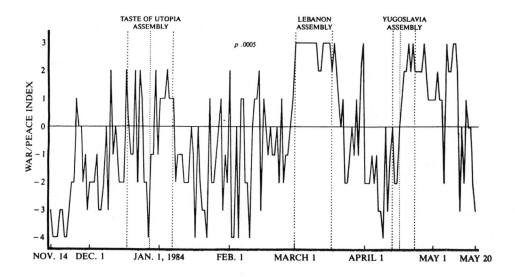

For the six-month period from November 13, 1983, to May 18, 1984, the daily level of the Lebanon Peace/War Index fluctuated widely and was generally negative. In contrast, during the three creating coherence assemblies held at this time (while the number of participants exceeded the predicted threshold for an influence on the war) there were plateau periods of progress toward peaceful resolution of this conflict. Time series analysis indicates significantly greater progress toward peace during these assemblies than would have been expected from the prior history of the Lebanon war (p = .000046). (Data source: daily Beirut newspapers, Al Nahar, Al Anwar, Le Reveil, and L'Orient.)

Reference: C.N. Alexander, T.M. Abou Nader, K.L. Cavanaugh, J.L. Davis, M.C. Dillbeck, R.J. Kfoury, D.W. Orme-Johnson, "Effects of the Maharishi Technology of the Unified Field on the Conflict in Lebanon: A Time Series Analysis of the Influence of International and National Creating Coherence Assemblies," *Scientific Research on the Transcendental Meditation and TM-Sidhi Program: Collected Papers*, Vol. 4, in press, (MIU Press, 1985).

This is astonishing! Have these effects been repeated?

Yes, twice a year since the first Taste of Utopia Assembly thousands of experts in the Maharishi Technology of the Unified Field have assembled together to produce this powerful influence of positivity for the whole world. The research on these assemblies shows decreased international conflicts, improved economic conditions, decreased infectious disease and accident rates, and improved harmonious relations all over the world.

Can you make this effect permanent?

Yes, we can by establishing one group of 7000 experts in the Maharishi Technology of the Unified Field in one place on earth. Actually, for insurance, one group of 7000 on each continent would be good.

What that means is that it is now within our reach to bring enlightenment and invincibility, peace and prosperity to ourselves and to all the people of the world.

We can do it in one stroke.

We live in a very great, fortunate time.

I'll take it!

Maharishi National Capitals of the Age of Enlightenment

Listed below are a few of the more than 200 Capitals throughout North America. For the one nearest you, call or write the one on this list that is closest to you.

**National Capital of the
Age of Enlightenment
For the United States**
5000 14th St. NW
Washington, D.C. 20011
(202) 723-9111

**National Capital of the
Age of Enlightenment
For Canada**
Box 6500, Huntsville
Ontario, P0A 1K0
(705) 635-2203

Maharishi Regional Capitals of the Age of Enlightenment

**Capital of the
Age of Enlightenment**
1601 N. Main Street
Fairfield, IA 52556
(515) 472-6548

**Florida Capital of the
Age of Enlightenment**
Box 967
Avon Park, FL 33825
(813) 452-2277

**St. Louis Capital of the
Age of Enlightenment**
Star Rte. #1, Box 129
Ste. Genevieve, MO 63670
(314) 756-5764

**Kansas City Capital of the
Age of Enlightenment**
Rural Rte. #1
Waverly, MO 64096
(816) 493-2285

**Dallas Capital of the
Age of Enlightenment**
Rural Rte. #1, Box 208
Forestburg, TX 76239
(817) 964-2224

**Houston Capital of the
Age of Enlightenment**
Rural Rte. #1, Box 468
Navasota, TX 77868
(409) 825-7926

**Capital of the Age
of Enlightenment**
Box 370
Livingston Manor, NY 12758
(914) 439-4310

**Capital of the Age
of Enlightenment**
P.O. Box 3
Lancaster, MA 01523
(617) 368-8660

**Capital of the
Age of Enlightenment
for Northern California**
Hwy. 175, Cobb, CA 95426
(707) 928-5213

**California Capital of the
Age of Enlightenment**
17310 Sunset Blvd.
Pacific Palisades, CA 90272
(213) 459-6477

**Caribbean Capital of the
Age of Enlightenment**
M.I.C.I., Box 1186, Las Croabas
Fajardo, Puerto Rico 00648
(809) 863-6010

**Maharishi
International University**
Fairfield, IA 52556
(515) 472-5031

Maharishi Vedic University
1111 H Street NW
Washington, D.C. 20005
(202) 737-1166

Maharishi City Capitals of The Age of Enlightenment

**Atlanta Capital of the
Age of Enlightenment**
3615 North Stratford NE
Atlanta, GA 30342
(404) 231-1093

**Austin Capital of the
Age of Enlightenment**
3103 Bee Caves Rd., #125
Austin, TX 78746
(512) 328-0871

**Cambridge Capital of the
Age of Enlightenment**
33 Garden Street
Cambridge, MA 02138
(617) 876-4581

**Chicago Capital of the
Age of Enlightenment**
3124 N. Southport
Chicago, IL 60657
(312) 477-0102

**Cleveland Capital of the
Age of Enlightenment**
20670 Center Ridge Rd.
Rocky River, OH 44116
(216) 333-6700

**Denver Capital of the
Age of Enlightenment**
1275 Franklin
Denver, CO 80218
(303) 861-5111

**Edmonton Capital of the
Age of Enlightenment**
10143 112th Street
Edmonton, Alberta T5K 1M1
(403) 424-5534

**Minneapolis Capital of the
Age of Enlightenment**
2700 University Ave. W.
St. Paul, MN 55114
(612) 641-0925

**Montreal Capital of the
Age of Enlightenment**
4205 St. Denis, Suite 210
Montreal, Quebec H2J 2K9
(514) 286-1501

**New York City Capital of
the Age of Enlightenment**
12 W. 21st Street, 9th Floor
New York, NY 10010
(212) 645-0202

**Ottawa Capital of the
Age of Enlightenment**
119 Queen St., Suite 404
Ottawa, Ontario K1P 6L8
(613) 234-7000

**Philadelphia Capital of the
Age of Enlightenment**
234 S. 22nd Street
Philadelphia, PA 19103
(215) 732-8464

**San Francisco Capital of the
Age of Enlightenment**
767 10th Ave.
San Francisco, CA 94118
(415) 668-1274

**Seattle Capital of the
Age of Enlightenment**
4317 Linden Ave. N.
Seattle, WA 98103
(206) 547-7527

**Toronto Capital of the
Age of Enlightenment**
1216 Yonge St., Suite 100
Toronto, Ontario M4T 1W1
(416) 964-1725

**Vancouver Capital of the
Age of Enlightenment**
6076 East Blvd.
Vancouver, B.C. V6M 3V5
(604) 263-2655

**Washington D.C. Capital of
the Age of Enlightenment**
2127 Leroy Pl. NW
Washington, D.C. 20008
(202) 387-5050

**West Los Angeles Capital of
the Age of Enlightenment**
17310 Sunset Blvd.
Pacific Palisades, CA 90272
(213) 459-3522

Maharishi Ayurveda Medical Centers

17308 Sunset Blvd.
Pacific Palisades, CA 90272
(213) 454-5531

P.O. Box 282
Fairfield, IA 52556
(515) 472-5866

2112 F Street N.W., Suite 503
Washington, D.C. 20037
(202) 785-2700

Maharishi Ayurveda Health Center for Behavioral Medicine and Stress Management

679 George Hill Road
Lancaster, MA 01523
(617) 365-4549